Advance P

"With certain events in the 60s, they say if you remember them, you weren't there. Well, David Chudwin was there and he remembers it all. From the music and the ever-changing social and political climate, to the first mission to land on the Moon, we gain a front-row seat to moments from the late 60s into the early 70s – one of the most pivotal times in American history."

FRANCIS FRENCH, author and *Los Angeles Times* bestselling coauthor of *Falling to Earth*

"David Chudwin and I were both blessed to have come of age during this amazing decade and to share the collective experience of that time. No other period produced such significant advances in medicine, technology, space travel, social justice and music. Dave was truly both a witness and a participant in the history that shaped much of that Miracle Decade. Those years not only changed the direction of our country, as well as much of the world, but continue to shape them today."

MARVIN RUBENSTEIN, PhD, author of *Apollo Memories*

"The Magical Decade *delivers that rarest of experiences –
a personalized, immersive tour of one of the most exciting,
tumultuous and impactful spans in American history.
From a Beatles concert to anti-war protests, to pop culture
to the historic launch of Apollo 11, David Chudwin was there
and absorbing it all, pushing himself ringside to capture the
essence of a transformative era. The result is a memoir, seen
through the astonishingly curious eyes of a young man,
which reads like a fireplace conversation with a friend."*

ROBERT KURSON, *New York Times*
bestselling author of *Shadow Divers* and *Rocket Men*

*"For any American who came of age in the turbulent 1960s
and 1970s,* The Magical Decade *will bring back a torrent
of memories. And thanks to author David Chudwin's good
fortune to personally experience many key moments in
the ten-year period he covers, readers will benefit from his
personal reflections 50 years later on this slice of history.
Baby Boomers like me, especially those captivated by popular
culture and the Space Race, will find fascinating details of
major events now remembered in much broader terms.*
The Magical Decade *offers a nostalgic rollercoaster ride
through the most formative period of Chudwin's life. His
narrative not only covers all the touchstones of the era, such
as Vietnam, the Moon landing and Watergate, but also
transformative developments in medicine and technology.
And, for younger readers, it also provides a valuable
historical perspective as the US continues to evolve."*

JOHN BISNEY, Former correspondent, CNN

This book is dedicated to my children,
Adam and Stacy,
to my granddaughter, Callie,
and is in memory of my wife, Claudia

Published by
LID Publishing
An imprint of LID Business Media Ltd.
The Record Hall, Studio 304,
16-16a Baldwins Gardens,
London EC1N 7RJ, UK

info@lidpublishing.com
www.lidpublishing.com

A member of:

businesspublishersroundtable.com

© David Chudwin, 2024
© LID Business Media Limited, 2024

Printed by Pelikan Basım
ISBN: 978-1-915951-23-6
ISBN: 978-1-915951-24-3 (ebook)

Cover and Page design: Caroline Li

THE
MAGICAL
DECADE

A personal memoir
and popular history
of **1965-75**

DAVID CHUDWIN MD

MADRID | MEXICO CITY | LONDON
BUENOS AIRES | BOGOTA | SHANGHAI

Contents

Introduction

In the wonderful 1994 fictional movie *Forrest Gump*, the title character, played by Tom Hanks, is in the middle of everything happening in the United States in the 1950s through 1980s. For those unfamiliar with the film, these events range from growing up with Elvis Presley, to meeting Presidents Kennedy and Johnson, to serving in Vietnam, to witnessing the Watergate break-in which led to President Nixon's resignation. Of course, all these episodes are fictional, a plot device to develop the character of Forrest Gump. They were filmed for the movie with computer-generated imagery, archival footage and special effects advanced for 1994.

I am certainly not Forrest Gump. I don't have a Southern drawl, I don't run very fast, and I have a different life story. What we do have in common, though, is that for a period during my formative years, from ages 15 to 25 years old, I was present at a variety of historical events.

I am a 'Baby Boomer,' the post-World War II generation born between 1946 and 1964 (I was born in 1950). There are more than 76 million of us.[1] We have lived during a time of revolutionary upheavals. **While other generations faced challenges, my generation went through a period of unprecedented social, political and cultural changes in almost every endeavour.** This book is about the enormity of those changes during a particular decade and how they affected me during that crucial decade of my development.

I call the years 1965–1975 **The Magical Decade**. The years I selected are somewhat arbitrary. (I know that technically the time span should be 1965–1974 to constitute a decade.) However, a combination of good timing, good luck and good instincts led me to be a participant in many of the great events of that particular time. Unlike the fictional Forrest Gump, I was actually there in person – I was often an eyewitness to history.

The Magical Decade began in earnest for me in August 1965 when I attended The Beatles concert at Comiskey Park in Chicago at the height of the British Invasion.[2] I was entering my sophomore year of high school at age 15 and my family was moving from Chicago to the suburbs that month. The world was a very different place then – the Vietnam War was raging, the battle for civil rights was the major American domestic issue, there were no personal computers or mobile phones, and social media did not exist.

Ten years later in 1975, I had graduated high school and then the University of Michigan in Ann Arbor and was attending medical school there. I was well on my way to becoming a physician. However, it had been a tumultuous decade, which deeply affected me and my fellow Baby Boomers. The Vietnam War was over, progress had been made in civil rights, men had landed on the Moon, and there had been great technological and medical advances. There were major cultural shifts in music, television, movies, plays, books, fashion and design. **I contend that there were more changes in more fields during The Magical Decade than perhaps during any other decade in American history.**

What follows is a personal memoir of 1965–1975. It is not a formal history of the era, nor is it an autobiography.

It is the reminiscences of a decade by topic as seen through my eyes – as I experienced it – with necessary historical context. While these events were many years ago, they had a profound impact on me then, as well as today. To me, these memories are still vivid and immediate and, as you will see, in many ways still relevant both to me and our world today. I am writing this book for my children and grandchildren, as well as my fellow Baby Boomers. I hope you enjoy this journey backwards in time with me.

FIG I-1: The author at Disney World in Florida in 1974 near the end of The Magical Decade. Note the bushy hair and the chequered white trousers. (Photo credit - David Chudwin)

CHAPTER 1

August 1965: The music

When I was growing up, music was a centre point of American culture, especially for young people my age. Listening to music on transistor radios and later audio cassettes was a daily habit. Record albums were played on analogue record players (with arms, needles and grooves on the discs) and then collected. Various pop musical genres were featured on commercial radio stations with engaging disc jockeys aiming for high ratings among the coveted teenage and young adult audiences. The higher the ratings, the more radio stations could charge for commercials aired between songs.

The early 1960s American music scene was an amalgam of folk music such as The Weavers and The Kingston Trio, country music including Elvis Presley and Loretta Lynn, and American pop groups such as The Four Seasons and Jan and Dean.

However, the start of The Magical Decade in the mid-1960s marked the rise of the musical British Invasion.[2] The 1960s had begun with surfer songs from American groups like The Beach Boys, especially popular from 1962–1964. But then a new musical wave appeared in America from across the Atlantic. The British Invasion was revolutionary, internationalizing rock and roll. British musicians took their sounds from more edgy American blues and jazz and adapted them to British themes. They then exported their musical product back to the United States by touring and recording albums.

In England a group called The Beatles was founded in 1960 with John Lennon, Paul McCartney, and George Harrison at the core; drummer Ringo Starr was added in 1962. They had their first hit song, "Love Me Do," at the end of 1962. Their 1963 number one hit "She Loves You" sold more than a million copies and held the record for the fastest-selling song in the UK until 1978.

By the time they first visited the US in February 1964 and appeared on *The Ed Sullivan Show*, 'Beatlemania' had swept the world. They had a string of number one hits, and their first movie, *A Hard Day's Night*, debuted soon after in July 1964.

The Beatles' first appearance in my hometown of Chicago, which I missed, was at the indoor Chicago Amphitheater in September 1964, but then they announced a second concert to be held at the baseball stadium, Comiskey Park, on 20 August 1965. Tickets sold out almost immediately.

My uncle, Mike Victor, was in the music business; he owned a record and music store on State Street in Madison, Wisconsin, just adjacent to the University of Wisconsin. Through his business connections, he was able to get four tickets to the upcoming concert for his two sons, Steve and Bob, and graciously gave the other two to me and my younger brother, Jeff. I had just turned 15 years old. I couldn't believe it! I had one of the hottest tickets in America. I was going to hear the English musical group The Beatles live in my hometown of Chicago.

Comiskey Park was a steel and concrete structure built on the South Side of Chicago in 1910. It was the home of the Chicago White Sox baseball team (as opposed to the Chicago Cubs, based in Wrigley Field on the North Side). Torn down in 1990, Comiskey Park was already one of the oldest baseball fields in the US when I went that day to see The Beatles.

The Beatles flew in from Houston, Texas, at 3 am Friday morning. They arrived at the smaller Midway Airport; police had ordered them to land there instead of the main O'Hare Airport because of fears that crowds there would disrupt the airport.

We attended the 3 pm performance. Our seats were on the upper level, far from the stage on the field, but we had good views of the scene. Tickets were priced at $2.50, $4.50 and $5.50, equivalent to approximately $24, $44 and $53 in 2023 dollars. I believe we had the $4.50 tickets.

We drove to Comiskey Park, parked in one of the large concrete lots, and climbed the long ramps to the upper deck, getting there about an hour before the performance was scheduled to start. The stadium steadily filled up until there was a crowd of more than 25,000 people. There were people of all ages, but a majority of the attendees seemed to be teenage girls who were truly fanatic Beatles fans.

"Who's your favourite Beatle?" was a common question at the time, with John and Paul the most frequent answers. Personally, my answer was Paul McCartney and I have remained a fan of Sir Paul for over five decades (my late wife and I attended his marathon 2011 concert at Wrigley Field).

Back in 1965, there were three brief opening acts before The Beatles arrived with a Chicago police motorcade escort. There were more police surrounding the perimeter inside Comiskey Park to prevent fans from rushing the field. The Beatles ran to the stage located in the middle of the stadium to the rapturous screams of thousands of young teenage girls and the enthusiastic applause of the rest of us.

As the band started to play, the raucous screams continued incessantly. One of my main memories of the concert was my annoyance at how these screams during the performance made it difficult to actually hear the music, despite the many loudspeakers.

The set list for the early show we attended has been lost to posterity, but the list of songs for the 8 pm show survives:[3]

1. "Twist and Shout"
2. "Baby's in Black"
3. "She's a Woman"
4. "I Feel Fine"
5. "Dizzy Miss Lizzy"
6. "Ticket to Ride"
7. "Everybody's Tryin' to Be My Baby"
8. "Can't Buy Me Love"
9. "I Wanna Be Your Man"
10. "A Hard Day's Night"
11. "Help!"
12. "I'm Down"

The concert was thrilling to me. I felt lucky to be there (thanks, Uncle Mike!). It was fun to be part of what seemed at the time to be a revolution in music. The excitement was palpable, even though the screaming girls were a bit much.

The Beatles remained the number one band in the world, with 17 number one hits and an additional 11 in the Top 10. Each new album was awaited with great anticipation, with fans even camping overnight outside record stores to be the first to purchase the new vinyl records (I was willing to wait a couple of days until the records were more easily obtainable). The group broke up for all practical purposes in April 1970 when Paul announced he was quitting.

The Beatles progressed musically from the simple three-chord songs of their early albums to musically complex songs augmented with masterful mixing by their producer, George Martin. They pioneered multitrack recording, use of classical instruments in pop songs, the addition of Asian Indian music, backward tracks and themed albums.

Of course, The Beatles were only part of the British Invasion. In 1965, when I was 15, my family moved from a house on the South Side of Chicago to the suburbs, a small village called Olympia Fields, where I attended Rich Township Central High School. 'Sock hops' were an important part of the high school social scene. These were dances in the school gymnasium. No shoes were allowed (so as not to damage the wooden basketball floor) and everyone walked around in their socks, hence the name. During the sock hops I tried to dance but was never very good at it.

My memories of the British Invasion music hits of the era are indelibly linked to memories of these sock hops – Eric Burdon and The Animals' "House of the Rising Sun" and "We Gotta Get Out of this Place"; The Kinks' "All Day and All of the Night" and "You Really Got Me"; The Who's "My Generation" and "Magic Bus"; The Hollies' "Bus Stop"; and last but not least, The Rolling Stones' "Street Fighting Man" and "Satisfaction," among many other of their number one hits from the mid-1960s.

These songs are the soundtrack of my life. They elicit deep nostalgia and even flashbacks to the time more than half a century ago when I was young. 'Oldies' radio stations are so popular because the music they play carries Baby Boomers like me back to their youths. The music also reminds me of how socially awkward I was as a 15-year-old sophomore in high school.

The Rolling Stones were probably the second most influential British band after The Beatles. In the beginning, they wore preppy suits and were not part of the drug scene. This changed in August 1964 when American troubadour Bob Dylan allegedly turned them on to marijuana. It was not until later that they experimented with a panoply of drugs, including LSD and even heroin.[4]

In contrast to the clean-cut Beatles in the mid-1960s, The Rolling Stones cultivated an image of rock's bad boys. "They weren't nice like The Beatles. They were shaggy, sulky and they pouted," wrote Robert Gore-Langton in 2012 in *The Express* on the 50th anniversary of their first performance.[4] They achieved bad boy status with drug use (exemplified by Keith Richards' alleged heroin addiction), marital infidelity (Mick Jagger had eight children by five different women), the sexual innuendo of some of their lyrics ["(I Can't Get No) Satisfaction"], and deliberate 'bad boy' marketing by their manager, Andrew Oldham.

I did not see The Rolling Stones in person until their United Center concert in Chicago on 25 January 2006, which I attended with my wife, Claudia, and my two children, who were 19 and 21 at the time. The Stones put on a rollicking performance with Mick Jagger in fine physical form for a 52-year-old man. The sound was so loud in the enclosed arena that I could barely hear when I left the United Center; I date my high-frequency hearing loss to that concert.

British rocker Elton John also began a musical career lasting half a century during The Magical Decade. Sir Elton was known for his flamboyant wardrobe, dramatic stage performances and his publicly gay persona. He teamed with lyricist Bernie Taupin to produce one hit after another in the 1970s and 1980s. Some of his early hits included "Border Song" (1970), "Tiny Dancer" (1971), "Rocketman" (1972), and "Candle in the Wind" (1974, and 1997 in memory of Princess Diana, a friend of his). After The Magical Decade, Sir Elton raised hundreds of millions of dollars to support AIDS/HIV research and treatment.

I did not hear Elton John live until 1982, after The Magical Decade, at the Civic Auditorium in San Francisco, as I was ending my medical fellowship training. At the concert he wore sequined outfits, outlandish wide glasses and jumped on the piano while destroying an electric guitar. My wife, Claudia, and I saw a more mature Sir Elton playing live at Wrigley Field in Chicago in a joint concert with Billy Joel in 2009. We were ticketed to see him again in October 2018 at the United Center in Chicago, but Claudia unexpectedly passed away in August; it was bittersweet to attend his performance with my daughter, Stacy.

The British rock band Queen also began a series of hits at the end of The Magical Decade. They released their first album *Queen* in 1973 and then exploded with the album *Night at the Opera* in 1975. The latter featured "Bohemian Rhapsody," a six-minute mock opera that was at the top of the charts in England for weeks. The band toured briefly in the US beginning in 1974 before they became famous; I never had the chance to see them live. I especially was a fan of Sir Brian May who, besides being a rock guitarist, also has a Ph.D. in astrophysics, one of my interests.

At the same time as the British Invasion, American music was also changing. At the forefront, Bob Dylan, who had turned The Beatles and The Rolling Stones on to marijuana, was leading a rebellion of homegrown folk and rock music. His songs "Blowin' in the Wind" (1963) and "The Times They Are a Changin'" (1964) served as anthems for the civil rights and anti-Vietnam War movements. Other groups such as the folk music trio Peter, Paul and Mary released best-selling covers of Dylan's songs. His music and writings were so influential that he won the Nobel Prize in Literature in 2016, the first musician to do so.

The high point of American popular music during The Magical Decade was the Woodstock Music and Art Fair in August 1969. That summer, while in college, I had a coveted seasonal job at an upscale men's clothing store on Michigan Avenue in Chicago. I was cautioned I could take off only one week during the summer. I had heard about a massive music festival planned for New York in August, but at the same time I was trying to get NASA press credentials to cover Apollo 11 in Florida in July (see Chapter 9). I was faced with a dilemma – music or space? I decided on space because I figured there would always be other musical events, but the first attempt to land on the Moon was special.

Woodstock turned out to be not just any music festival. Planned at first for 50,000 attendees, over 400,000 people showed up at Max Yasgur's dairy farm near Bethel, New York to hear 32 musical acts play on 15–18 August. Marred by rainstorms, traffic jams and logistical nightmares, the peaceful crowd was treated to iconic performances by Jimi Hendrix, Janis Joplin, Jefferson Airplane, Creedence Clearwater Revival, Joe Cocker, Richie Havens, Crosby, Stills & Nash, and many others. Most of these performances reflected the social issues of 1969. The event and many performances were captured in an Academy Award-winning documentary *Woodstock* the next year, along with a best-selling soundtrack album, a favourite of mine.

Woodstock was emblematic of the great changes that had occurred in American pop music in the 1960s during The Magical Decade. The gentle harmonic sounds of The Beach Boys gave way to gritty songs by artists such as Janis Joplin. Woodstock epitomized the revolution in American music and society, and its sounds had a long-lasting influence on music in the decades following it.

While Bob Dylan did not appear at Woodstock, I did see Dylan perform in person toward the end of The Magical Decade on 2 February 1974, at Crisler Arena in Ann Arbor when I was in medical school. Even at that time, he was a musical legend. Dylan's nasal voice was distinctive as he played a lengthy concert with his main backup group, The Band.

The set list for the event was long and varied. Some of these were among my favourite Dylan songs – for example, "The Times They Are A-Changin," "Don't Think Twice," and "It Ain't Me Babe." However, it was also a special treat to hear him with The Band, who had produced hits of their own, such as "The Night They Drove Old Dixie Down."

The crowd was enthusiastic, and a fair percentage was high on marijuana or other drugs. The concert lasted three hours and those of us who were there thought it was well worth the $8.50 ticket price (equivalent to $55 in 2023 dollars).

Besides Dylan, some of my other beloved American singers released songs in the early 1970s. Among folk artists, Paul Simon and Art Garfunkel had a successful joint career but split up in 1970 after five award-winning duo albums. Paul then released solo albums in 1972 (*Paul Simon*) and 1973 (*There Goes Rhymin' Simon*), the latter including "Kodachrome" and "American Tune," two of my favourites.

While I was in general not a big country music fan, I did appreciate Dolly Parton, who started her musical career as a songwriter and then a performer at the beginning of The Magical Decade. She released her most popular and enduring songs "Jolene" in 1973 and "I Will Always Love You" in 1974. There have been subsequently many covers of these two songs by other artists, most notably her goddaughter Miley Cyrus performing "Jolene" and Whitney Houston's bravura performance of "I Will Always Love You."

Of course, the biggest country star of all-time, Elvis Presley, made a comeback during The Magical Decade. His December 1968 television special *Elvis* revitalized his career. Presley's iconic record album, *Elvis in Memphis,* was released in June 1969 and the next month he began the first of a long series of lucrative month-long residencies at the newly opened International Hotel in Las Vegas.

Two of the most popular songwriters of the early 1970s were married to each other for a while – James Taylor and Carly Simon. Taylor temporarily overcame addiction to drugs to release his first album, containing "Carolina in My Mind," in February 1969 in the US. His breakthrough album the next year was *Sweet Baby James*, and I still have my copy of the vinyl record in my collection. His soft folk rock style of music dominated the early 1970s.

He married fellow singer-songwriter Carly Simon in 1972 and they performed on each other's albums. Carly Simon's most successful songs were "Anticipation" (1971) and "You're So Vain" (1972). The two divorced in 1983. Taylor quit his heroin addiction afterwards during his second marriage, has remained clean and has continued to perform.

Taylor and Simon were both friends and musical collaborators with Carole King, whose album *Tapestry,* released in 1971, sold more than 25 million copies and won four Grammy Awards, including Album of the Year. Like Dolly Parton, Carole King has been a prolific and successful songwriter whose tunes have been covered by other performers. For example, Aretha Franklin's hit "(You Make Me Feel Like) A Natural Woman" was composed by Carole King, as was "You've Got a Friend" performed by James Taylor. King has written or cowritten more than 118 songs that made the Billboard Top 100 list through the years.

I was also able to attend other concerts in person in Ann Arbor between 1968 and 1975, my final year of medical school. Some of the memorable ones ranged from the pop music group Fifth Dimension to renowned classical pianist Vladimir Horowitz playing on a Sunday afternoon on 20 April 1975 in a piano recital at Hill Auditorium.

Besides rock music, Ann Arbor was also the home – while I lived there – to the first Ann Arbor blues and jazz festivals. The premiere event was in August 1969 and was known as the Ann Arbor Blues Festival. The concerts were held on a stage in Gallup Park, along the Huron River. Legendary bluesmen headlined the concert, including Howlin' Wolf, Muddy Waters, Otis Rush and B.B. King, among many others. The festival was sponsored by the University of Michigan and Canterbury House, a ministry of the Episcopal Church and a haven for music.

I remember the 1969 event not only for the music, but also because I was stuck at the end of the concert with no way to get back to my apartment in central Ann Arbor. For the only time in my life, I decided to hitchhike back, figuring that with all the students there, someone would have pity on me. Of course, this was entirely against my upbringing in Chicago where, even in that era, hitchhikers would be robbed or worse. Luckily, I made it back home in one piece.

There was a second festival in 1970, but it was not as successful, losing money. The University of Michigan ended its sponsorship and there was no festival in 1971.

The event was reborn as the Ann Arbor Blues & Jazz Festival in 1972. It aimed at a wider audience by including jazz and featuring commercial artists such as Ray Charles and Miles Davis. I also attended the 1973 festival and saved the program, which cost 25 cents ($1.70 in 2023 dollars). (FIG 1-2).

FIG 1-2: Program for the 1973 Ann Arbor Blues & Jazz Festival from the collection of David Chudwin. (Photo credit - David Chudwin)

Controversial cultural and political radical John Sinclair was responsible for the resurrection of the festival in 1972–1974 but it lost money and he was unable to find a suitable venue after Ann Arbor refused use of city parks. The Ann Arbor Blues & Jazz Festival was then dormant until it was revived again in a different, largely indoor format from 1992–2006.

I was privileged to listen to some veteran blues pioneers at the 1969, 1972 and 1973 events. Afterwards, musicians T-Bone Walker died in 1975, Howlin' Wolf passed away in 1976, and Muddy Waters in 1983. The Ann Arbor Blues & Jazz Festival returned to life in 2017 as an outdoor event and has been held yearly since then.

If the exciting British Invasion marked the start of The Magical Decade in the 1960s, disco gradually crept into the music scene in the early 1970s toward the end of The Magical Decade. Clubs called discotheques became popular in large cities such as Los Angeles and New York. The first disco mega-star was Gloria Gaynor, later to be followed by Donna Summer and the Bee Gees.

I personally disliked disco music as a genre even while admiring some of the artists. Although it occurred outside The Magical Decade, the infamous Disco Demolition Night on 12 July 1979 epitomized the disdain of many Americans for disco. The event was planned as a publicity stunt between a double-header Chicago White Sox baseball game at Comiskey Park in Chicago, the venue where I had heard The Beatles play in 1965.

Fans who disliked disco brought disco albums and records to the ballpark. A crate of records was exploded by the organizers in centre field. The crowd of 50,000, many of whom were inebriated, became unruly and many rushed the field. Riot police needed to be called in to restore order. The White Sox had to forfeit the second game to the Detroit Tigers due to damage to the field.

The Magical Decade ended in 1975 with these songs at the top of the 1975 pop charts:[5]

1. "Love Will Keep Us Together"– Captain & Tennille
2. "Rhinestone Cowboy"– Glen Campbell
3. "Philadelphia Freedom"– Elton John
4. "Before the Next Teardrop Falls" – Freddy Fender
5. "My Eyes Adored You" – Frankie Valli
6. "Shining Star" – Earth, Wind & Fire
7. "Fame" – David Bowie

In retrospect, the 1960s and 70s were a revolutionary period for a variety of different types of popular music, especially during The Magical Decade. When hearing the music now, Baby Boomers like me are transported back to their youthful years. The era was headlined in America by the British Invasion and then by Woodstock in 1969. Beyond that singular event, The Beatles, The Rolling Stones, Bob Dylan and other artists will go down in music history. I had a chance to hear them live in concerts, which I vividly remember five decades later.

CHAPTER 2

August 1965: Civil rights - unfulfilled promises

In the presence of Congressional leaders of both parties, President Lyndon B. Johnson, on 6 August 1965, signed the landmark Voting Rights Act of 1965. This historic law removed obstacles to voting by Black Americans and other minorities. No longer would literacy tests and poll taxes be allowed to suppress basic voting rights.

The struggle to achieve voting rights for Black people was a long and bitter one. White segregationists in the South vehemently opposed giving the ballot, and thereby power, to the sons and daughters of former African-American slaves. The fight over voting rights came to a head in March 1965 during 'Bloody Sunday.'

On 7 March 1965, Hosea Williams and John Lewis led 600 marchers from Selma, Alabama, toward Montgomery, the Alabama State Capitol, to press for voting rights. It was the beginning of The Magical Decade and the main goal then of the civil rights movement was to secure the right to vote for African-Americans.

As they crossed the Edmund Pettus Bridge in Selma, the unarmed, peaceful demonstrators were attacked by Alabama State Police troopers with billy clubs, whips and tear gas.[6] Fifty-eight protestors were treated at hospitals, including John Lewis, who suffered a fractured skull. Years later, Lewis became a respected Congressman.

I was 14 years old. The photos and television video of the unprovoked attack on the nonviolent demonstrators deeply disturbed me at the time. How could police treat their fellow citizens with such violence and hatred? Of course, it was all about race – the Alabama troopers were all White and the marchers were largely African-Americans.

Racial tensions in the US both then and now are a lingering legacy of slavery and the Civil War. While there have been great strides taken, racial inequality in jobs, housing, health care and education remains one of the great contradictions in American society. The law promises equal justice, but for centuries there have been discrepancies in policing, law enforcement, sentencing and prison confinement between Black people and other citizens.

The first African slaves in America were brought to the Jamestown settlement in 1619. They were used as a source of cheap labour for farming plantations, primarily in the Southern US. By the time of the Civil War, there were an estimated four million Black individuals in captivity. The Emancipation Proclamation by President Abraham Lincoln in 1862 set them free as of 1 January 1863. Of course, it took the North's victory in 1865 against the slave-owning Confederacy in the Civil War to allow this to occur. The last slaves to gain emancipation were freed in Texas on "Juneteenth" (19 June) 1865.

The Reconstruction Era (1865–1877) was the attempt to bring the defeated Southern states back into the Union and to liberate the slaves and give them basic rights. However, there was a violent backlash against bringing the freed African-Americans into society in the South and border states. State legislatures enacted 'Jim Crow' laws to discriminate against the former slaves, setting up a system of segregation whereby African-Americans had inferior housing, schools and jobs. Vigilante groups, such as the White Ku Klux Klan, enforced segregation and used illegal lynchings to intimidate Black citizens to comply.

Prominent African-Americans such as Frederick Douglass, Booker T. Washington, W.E. B. Du Bois and Ida B. Wells struggled against discrimination, poverty and lynchings. However, the US Supreme Court, in a series of rulings beginning with the *Civil Rights Cases* of 1883, legalized segregation. The *Plessy v. Ferguson* decision in 1896 justified and codified segregation in society based on the "separate but equal" doctrine. Unfortunately, conditions were not equal, and the doctrine was used to justify discrimination.

By the 1920s, segregation was firmly in place in the South as a matter of law and local customs. Black people were prevented from voting and using the same public facilities as White people. Schools, parks, swimming pools, water fountains, beaches, housing, hospitals and employment were all separate for Blacks and Whites, but in fact unequal. Over 4,000 lynchings in the South from 1877 to 1950 were used to terrorize African-Americans and maintain White dominance. There were also race riots in cities such as Chicago (1919) and Tulsa (1921) during which thriving Black communities were attacked by angry Whites.

After World War I, large numbers of African-Americans started to migrate to cities in the North such as Detroit, Chicago, Philadelphia and New York. By 1919, an estimated one million Black people left the South for jobs and to escape 'Jim Crow' laws. While there was no legal segregation in the North, the migrants still faced discrimination. The jobs for men in factories, mills and foundries were often dirty and dangerous. Women sought coveted domestic jobs where they worked as maids for White families doing laundry, cooking, cleaning and taking care of children.

Segregation in the US Armed Forces continued during World War II, with separate Black contingents in the Army and Air Corps. The 92nd Infantry and 332nd Fighter Group (Tuskegee Airmen) served with particular distinction. Over 900,000 African-American men and women were members of the US military, almost all in segregated units.

The fighting ability, bravery and sacrifice of African-American citizens in World War II persuaded President Harry Truman to order an end to segregation in the Armed Forces in July 1948. Executive Order 9981 abolished discrimination "on the basis of race, color, religion or national origin."[7] Groups including the Urban League and National Association for the Advancement of Colored People (NAACP), and influential Black leaders, such as A. Philip Randolph, had lobbied for the change. There was some resistance from the military, especially the Army, but the need for troops in the Korean War necessitated integration of Army combat units.

When I was born in 1950, segregation was still legal in the South under the "separate but equal" doctrine. Even in the North, including Chicago where I grew up, there were racial disparities in housing, schools, health care and jobs. Black people in big cities were confined to largely dilapidated neighbourhoods, informally known as 'Black ghettos.' Local schools in these neighbourhoods were often inferior with older buildings, less experienced teachers and fewer teaching supplies.

In the early 1950s when I was growing up, use of the demeaning 'n word' was not uncommon. Television shows such as *Amos 'n' Andy* (1951–1960) promoted racial stereotypes of African-Americans. Blackface makeup was used by White people in minstrel shows, vaudeville and movies, despite its racist connotations. Racism, while official in the South, was also prevalent in other parts of the US.

My own introduction to African-Americans at about the age of four came through exposure to a Black housemaid, Ida, who came to work for us during the day. Our neighbourhood on the Far South Side of Chicago was segregated and there were virtually no Black people living there. I also did not have any Black children in my classes when I started school (FIG 2-1).

FIG 2-1: The author's second-grade classroom in 1958. Note that all the children were White.
(Photo credit - David Chudwin)

Ida cooked our dinners, washed and ironed my dad's shirts, and kept an eye on me and my two younger brothers before taking a bus back home at night. She was part of the family for about four years, until we moved to a different neighbourhood.

My parents trusted Ida enough that they allowed her to take me and my younger brothers to her own home when they travelled to Michigan for a long weekend for my father to go deer hunting. Meanwhile, we kids enjoyed staying at a house in a different neighbourhood, as well as Ida's cooking.

While Chicago had a growing, thriving Black community in the 1950s, housing for it was isolated to areas on the Near South Side and West Sides of town. Even as years passed, there were almost no Black families in the area where I grew up on the Far South Side. Similarly, the Chicago public grammar schools I attended (Warren, McDowell and Caldwell) had very few Black students. I do not remember having any Black friends as a child; this was not because of any racism on my part, but a reflection of the *de facto* housing segregation in Chicago in the 1950s.

The winds of change started to blow in 1954 when the US Supreme Court reversed past rulings and struck down segregation in the landmark *Brown vs. Board of Education of Topeka* ruling.[8] By a 9–0 unanimous decision, the Court decided that segregation violated the 14th Amendment to the US Constitution, which provided for equal protection under the law. Then in December 1955, an African-American seamstress, Rosa Parks, refused to give up her seat on a segregated bus in Montgomery, Alabama, and was arrested. The Black community of Montgomery, led by a young preacher named Martin Luther King, Jr., boycotted the buses for 381 days until December 1956, when the US Supreme Court upheld lower court rulings prohibiting segregation in the bus system and other public accommodations.

While school segregation had been outlawed, integration of schools in the South met with fierce opposition from segments of the White population, local politicians and, in the case of Arkansas, the state National Guard. Finally, in September 1957, nine Black teenagers entered Central High School in Little Rock, Arkansas, protected by federal marshals and troops.

Television nightly news brought dramatic pictures of the Little Rock showdown, including soldiers, some with bayonets, escorting the Black students to school. Protesters carrying Confederate flags yelled the 'n word' and other epithets at them. After being admitted to the school, the 'Little Rock Nine' continued to be subjected to racial taunts and harassment, including shoving and pushing by White students, but they persevered.

The sight of US troops with bayonets on one side and jeering White protesters on the other, with teenage Black students in between, unnerved me as a seven-year-old boy watching the news on television. I did not understand the need for the US Army to enforce court orders to allow these teenagers just to go to school, nor did I fathom the vehemence of Whites whose dominance was being challenged.

I and others in the North watched these events with concern. However, our lives were not as directly affected as those in the South, where local segregation persisted in restaurants, hotels, parks, beaches and, most importantly, in voter suppression. 'Freedom Riders,' who were young people of all races from the North, challenged these decades-old vestiges of segregation. Three of them, Michael Schwerner, James Chaney and Andrew Goodman, all of whom were White, were murdered in June 1964 in Mississippi, a crime that shocked the nation.

The March on Washington for Jobs and Freedom on 28 August 1963 was organized to press for an end to segregation and economic justice for African-Americans. More than 250,000 people crowded the National Mall in front of the Lincoln Memorial to hear speakers such as Dr Martin Luther King, Jr. and musical performers such as Peter, Paul and Mary. King gave his iconic "I Have a Dream" speech that still sends shivers up and down my spine, as it did that day when I watched it live on television as a 13-year-old boy.[9]

The march was important in exerting pressure on President Lyndon B. Johnson and Congress to pass the Civil Rights Act of 1964, which forbade discrimination based on race. However, there was still resistance in the South to voting rights, with literacy tests and poll taxes used to discourage Black people from voting.

The Southern Christian Leadership conference led by King planned a series of marches in Selma, Alabama, to promote voting and other rights. The 7 March 1965 march led to a violent attack by Alabama state troopers and vigilantes on the protesters that was vividly captured on national television and in pictures. 'Bloody Sunday' was a turning point as national opposition grew to Southern resistance and against violence against Blacks. The Voting Rights Act of 1965 was signed into law by President Johnson in August and prohibited poll taxes and literacy tests, and guaranteed the right to vote for all Americans.

It is ironic that, more than 50 years later, efforts to suppress voting by minorities are continuing with new laws and regulations passed by state legislatures after the disputed 2020 election.

Meanwhile, in the North, there were protests against *de facto* housing segregation. In 1966, my hometown of Chicago was the centre of attention. Dr Martin Luther King held a major rally on 10 July 1966, the day before I turned 16 years old. Over 35,000 attended the Chicago Freedom Movement gathering at Soldiers Field, which featured speeches by King and performances by

Stevie Wonder, Mahalia Jackson, and Peter, Paul and Mary. The movement held rallies outside real estate offices and organized marches into all-White neighbourhoods on the Southwest and Northwest Sides where they were met with open hostility.

I did not personally witness these marches because they were in different parts of Chicago than where I lived as a teenager. I do remember the anger of the White residents as shown on television and the determination of the Black protesters led by Dr King and their White and Hispanic allies. The real estate controversy dominated local television news I watched and the newspaper headlines I read each day.

The real estate industry in Chicago had played a role in housing discrimination by steering customers to specific neighbourhoods, depending on race. Some real estate contracts still had 'restrictive covenants' that prevented sales to African-Americans or other minorities.

A few unscrupulous real estate agents, known as 'blockbusters,' would try to profit by getting one or two Black families to move into a hitherto White neighbourhood. The agents would then sow false fears among the White residents concerning gangs and a drop in their property values in order to collect fast commissions from panic sales. While such illegal tactics expanded the areas into which Black people could move, blockbusting in fact actually promoted segregation.

In August 1966, negotiations were held between Chicago Freedom Movement leaders, City Hall officials and the Chicago Real Estate Board. An agreement was reached for open housing in Chicago, although more than 50 years later that dream has not been fully realized.

Personally, I had started high school in September 1964 at Bowen High School on the South Side of Chicago. The school population was mixed based on racial and socioeconomic bases. Among the White population were first-generation children of Eastern European Catholic descent; Jewish children; and 'greaser' gangs who, when out of school, wore white T-shirts with cigarette packs twisted in the sleeve. There were also a few Black and Latino students. There was a 'track' system in the Chicago Public Schools that had the effect of marginalizing minority students.

Meanwhile, in 1965, at the start of The Magic Decade, my parents were considering moving out of Chicago. Our family became part of 'White flight' from American cities to the suburbs. In August we moved to the small village of Olympia Fields, 23 miles south of our Chicago home. Our motives were not racial but an effort to improve our living conditions. There were many factors involved in the decision – the quest for better schools for myself and my two younger brothers, the desire for a bigger and more modern house, a search for more land than a crowded city lot, and concerns about gangs not too far from our Chicago neighbourhood (we lived on Blackstone Avenue, a couple of miles south of the infamous Blackstone Rangers gang territory).

The new house was modern, with high ceilings and more space, and it was situated on a large double lot totalling more than an acre. At that time, Olympia Fields was in the country, with well water and a Rural Route address (a post office was not built until a couple of years later). This contrasted with the often crowded, dilapidated three-story apartment buildings common in Chicago, along with old schools with large classes lacking air conditioning, modern equipment and supplies.

My new high school, Rich Township High School Central Campus, otherwise known as Rich Central, was only four years old when I entered in September 1965. The student body was almost homogeneously White, with few African-Americans or Latinos. Rich Central had an outstanding, mainly young, faculty. It had many extracurricular activities including sports and a plethora of clubs. It still had an 'honour system' with unlocked lockers when I first arrived.

I joined the sophomore track team as a shot putter. I wanted to be on a sports team, figuring that shot putting required the least athleticism from someone like myself with almost no athletic ability. I also joined the staff of *The Torch*, the high school newspaper, under the watchful eye of faculty advisor Mr Robert Dilworth. I participated in student council, eventually as vice president, and also acted in some plays. My favourite course was Junior English, taught by an inspiring teacher, Mr J.C. Dredla.

My senior year in 1968 was an *annus horribilis* – a terrible year – in the outside world. Dr King was assassinated in Memphis, Tennessee on 4 April and racial riots broke out in protest in many large cities, including Chicago. The next day rioting began on the West Side of Chicago. Police gunfire killed 11 and wounded 48, mainly African-Americans; 90 police officers were injured; and more than 2,000 people were arrested.

Large swathes of buildings along West Madison Street were burned down in the conflict. The National Guard was called up and US Army troops were deployed to restore order. The riots did not directly affect me because they occurred only in Chicago and not in the suburbs, but I did follow the news reports closely. However, months later I saw in person the destruction left behind on the West Side; it would take decades for the area to fully recover from the violence and devastation.

I understood the anger, but the violence in Chicago and elsewhere after King's death led to injuries and arrests of mainly Black people and destroyed a neighbourhood, which had provided jobs and housing to those who lived there. The mayhem seemed to me to be counterproductive to the cause.

Then in June, Senator Robert Kennedy was killed after winning the California presidential primary. I watched on our black-and-white television as he lay dying after being shot at the Ambassador Hotel in Los Angeles. Kennedy was popular among Blacks and Latinos and his death heightened anger in populations already reeling from the King assassination.

I had volunteered to campaign for Senator Eugene McCarthy's quest to win the 1968 Democratic nomination for president. I had felt betrayed by President Lyndon Johnson's escalation of the Vietnam War after running as the 'peace candidate' in 1964 (see Chapter 7). McCarthy's entrance into the race was one of the reasons that President Johnson decided not to run for another term, as he announced on 31 March 1968, in a surprise conclusion to a speech to the nation.

The 1968 Democratic National Convention was held in Chicago in August, but I had to leave the week before to start classes at the University of Michigan in Ann Arbor. I just missed the 'police riot' during which the police invaded the McCarthy headquarters and beat and arrested staffers there.

As a freshman in Ann Arbor in the fall of 1968, I decided to join the news staff of The Michigan Daily. Founded in 1893, The Daily is the independent student-run newspaper on campus. Generations of journalists learned their craft working on The Daily. I started off as an assistant news editor and reporter and ended as managing editor, the number three position in the hierarchy, in my senior year.

The student population in Ann Arbor was overwhelmingly White, with few African-American or Latino students. After the King assassination, Black student groups began to put pressure on the university's administration to increase Black admissions. However, progress was slow and late in 1969 several of these groups (Black Student Union, Black Law Student Alliance, Black Psychologists and Black Educational Caucus) joined together to negotiate with the administration.

University President Robben W. Fleming invited representatives of these groups, collectively known as the Black Action Movement (BAM), to a dinner meeting in February 1970. The BAM leaders put forth a series of demands, including 10% Black admissions by 1973–1974, a Black Student Center, increased scholarships for minority students, improvements in counselling and support services, and a Black Studies Program, among others. There was a demonstration on the lawn of the President's house in support of these demands.

As negotiations dragged on, BAM announced a campus-wide strike to begin 20 March 1970. There were class disruptions, picketing, blocking building entrances and demonstrations by BAM and its allied student groups. The strike lasted 18 days before a settlement was reached.

It was an exciting and scary time on campus. I covered some of the events for *The Daily*. One day I was at the Law School as strikers, mainly African-Americans, noisily entered the faculty office areas. I was dictating a story by telephone to *The Daily* from an office telephone when there was a commotion as police arrived. I flung down the telephone and fled to avoid the police onslaught before I could explain what was happening. I made my way back to the Student Publications Building at 420 Maynard, where I was met with warm greetings – the editors thought I had been arrested or worse.

Most students accepted the need for a strike and supported BAM's demands. Some objected to disruption of classes and their education. However, it was estimated that up to 75% of students were absent from undergrad LSA classes by the end of the strike. The successful student boycott, supported by a minority of faculty members, put pressure on the Board of Regents to urgently address the BAM demands. The Regents met in an emergency session with Fleming for 16 hours and then released a statement that 10% Black enrolment by 1973 was 'assured.'

On 1 April 1970, I was assigned to cover the BAM mass meeting in the Michigan Union Ballroom. Several hundred BAM members and supporters attended. The BAM negotiators there announced an agreement with the University administration on most of the demands and recommended ending the strike. The euphoric audience approved the recommendation by voice vote.

The large banner headline the next day read "BAM ENDS CLASS STRIKE, Accepts Regental Statement, by Dave Chudwin" (FIG 2-2). There was jubilation that the strike was over but also a grim realism that the BAM goals would be difficult to achieve. (Indeed, there were BAM protests again in 1975, 1987 and 2014).

FIG 2-2: The author wrote the lead article in *The Michigan Daily* about settlement of the Black Action Movement strike at the University of Michigan in 1970. (Photo credit - David Chudwin)

The BAM strike had national implications when Vice President Spiro T. Agnew criticized President Fleming for the agreement, calling it a "surrender" and a "callow retreat from reality."[10]

While at the University of Michigan, I had limited contact with African-American or Latino students. This was not the result of any prejudice but self-segregation. For example, there were traditionally all-Black fraternities and sororities. There was no overt discrimination, but vestiges of racism affected life on campus.

Two of the Black editors of *The Daily* I worked with closely later went on to illustrious careers. Alexa Canady (class of 1971) was Feature Editor of *The Daily*. She later received her MD degree from the University of Michigan and became the first African-American female neurosurgeon in history. She specialized in paediatric neurosurgery, the first African-American surgeon to do so, and was chief of neurosurgery at Children's Hospital of Michigan from 1987–2001 and professor of neuro-surgery at Wayne State University. Dr Canady has been cited nationally as being a positive role model for female and Black physicians.

Eugene Robinson (class of 1974) was the first Black Co-Editor-in-Chief of *The Michigan Daily*. He continued in journalism. He joined the staff of the *Washington Post* in 1980 and has become a respected liberal columnist, winning a Pulitzer Prize in 2009 for his columns about Barack Obama's run for the presidency. He was elected to the Pulitzer Prize Board in 2011 and was its chairman from 2017–2018. He has appeared frequently as a liberal commentator on political talk shows, including NBC's *Meet the Press* and various MSNBC broadcasts.

Looking back, The Magical Decade marked a turn-ing point in the quest for equality. It began in 1965 with the marches in Selma, Alabama, Bloody Sunday and the passage of the historic Voting Rights Act of 1965. The next year, Dr Martin Luther King started to lead pro-tests in the North, including my own city of Chicago, against housing discrimination. Until his assassination in 1968, he was one of the most important leaders of the civil rights movement. The riots in Chicago and other cities after his death destroyed inner city areas and created a further racial divide as National Guard and Army troops were mobilized to restore order.

Through the early 1970s, African-Americans made progress against prejudice in many spheres, including voting rights, political influence and power, professional advancement, and development of a Black middle class. Despite these improvements, by the end of The Magic Decade in 1975, there were still serious disparities between conditions for Whites and African-American individuals, which have persisted to the present day.

More recently, the 'Black Lives Matter' protests against racism in policing in 2020 harkened back to protests from The Magical Decade, more than half a century before. Civil rights will remain an issue as long as racism continues to rear its ugly head.

CHAPTER 3

December 1965: Religion - organized and unorganized

I went to Rome and the Vatican in 1970 as part of an informal six-week college trip abroad to Europe and the Middle East with my good friend, Mike Froman. Although not Catholic, we visited the historic and religious sites to better understand the culture of Italy. We attended a papal audience with Pope Paul VI to have an opportunity to see an important religious teacher in person.

The meeting was held in a large audience hall at Castel Gandolfo, a town in the hills about 25 km away from Rome. The scenic town was the summer abode of popes for centuries. There were hundreds of people present in the modern audience hall. The smiling Pope was carried in on a raised chair in a Mediaeval manner to cheers of "Viva il Papa," as flashbulbs popped from old-fashioned cameras (FIG 3-1). As a non-Catholic, the audience format then seemed formal and anti-quated, with little interaction between the pontiff and the attendees. Paul VI gave a brief welcome in several languages and then blessed the crowd. However, those in attendance were happy to have been in the presence of a historical religious figure.

FIG 3-1: Pope Paul VI photographed by the author at Castel Gandolfo, Italy in 1970.
(Photo credit - David Chudwin)

Four years earlier, Pope Paul VI had presided on 7 December 1965, over the conclusion of the Second Vatican Council; this was the main event in organized religion during the beginning of The Magical Decade. The meeting of over 2,500 Catholic bishops, priests and laypeople had been ordered by Pope John XXIII in 1959 to modernize the Catholic Church. The delegates began their deliberations in Rome in 1962 and the concluding session was in December 1965, presided over by Pope John's successor, Pope Paul VI.

The Council, the first in 100 years, produced 16 documents, which attempted to bring the Catholic Church into the modern world. The year 2012 marked the 50th anniversary of the opening of Vatican II and was a time to judge its significance. According to a 2012 NPR report about the Council, Georgetown University Professor Rev. O'Malley:

"says a theme of the documents was reconciliation. In keeping, they allowed for Catholics to pray with other Christian denominations, encouraged friendship with other non-Christian faiths, and opened the door for languages besides Latin to be used during Mass. Other new positions concerned education, the media and divine revelation."[11]

Also in 2012, Archbishop Gregory Aymond of New Orleans wrote:

"John XXIII saw Vatican II as a chance for renewal in the face of the 'signs of the times' and said he called the Council to open a window and let in fresh air. This resulted in reforms that made the church more accessible to the modern world, such as Mass in the vernacular and dialogue with other believers, and the openness of the Council was reflected in the presence of men and women religious, laypeople and even non-Catholics among its official observers."[12]

Among the other reforms, refraining from eating meat on Friday, as a form of penance, was made optional, although still encouraged.

The Council promoted dialogue with other Christian faiths, especially with the Greek Orthodox Church. On 7 December 1965, the centuries-old mutual excommunication of 1054 was lifted in a joint declaration by Pope Paul VI and Ecumenical Patriarch Athenagoras 1 of the Greek Orthodox Church.

Vatican II also addressed the relationship between the church and other religions. Specifically, the church's relationship with Jews was explored in the document *Nostra Aetate*, the fourth chapter of which states:

> "Given this great spiritual heritage common to Christians and Jews, it is the wish of this sacred Council to foster and recommend a mutual knowledge and esteem ... the Jews should not be presented as rejected by God or accursed, as though this follows from Scripture ... The Church ... deplores all hatred, persecution and other manifestations of antisemitism, whatever the period and whoever was responsible."[13]

Vatican II also addressed governance of the Church. The Council emphasized collegiality. While the bishops under the Pope retained spiritual and temporal authority, this was shared with members of religious orders and laypeople. There was an ongoing debate about the role of national conferences of bishops in this scheme.

Besides changes in the Catholic Church, the status of the Jewish religion in the modern world was also an important topic during The Magical Decade. The relationship between Judaism and its homeland in Israel was linked to two major wars involving Israel during that decade. The June 1967 Six-Day War saw Israel decisively defeat its Arab neighbours and gain territory from Syria (the Golan Heights), Egypt (the Sinai) and Jordan (the West Bank). The capture of East Jerusalem with its religious sites such as the Western (Wailing) Wall was especially meaningful to Jews in Israel and around the world.

I visited Israel in 1970 when I was 20 years old, and I was struck by the sense of optimism. The Israelis had triumphed over their Arab enemies and held a decisive military advantage. The Israeli economy was improving, and high technology was beginning to take hold in the scientific-industrial base. Tourists and pilgrims were easily able to visit religious sites such as the Western Wall, part of the Second Temple (FIG 3-2).

FIG 3-2: The Western (Wailing) Wall in Jerusalem as photographed by the author in 1970.
(Photo credit - David Chudwin)

By 1973, six years after the 1967 war, the military situation had changed due to the Yom Kippur War. Arab armies launched a surprise attack on 6 October 1973, on Israel during the country's holiest day. The Arabs made advances and caused Israeli casualties before they were turned back by the Israelis, assisted by American military weapons and supplies.

One result was the 1973–1974 oil embargo by the Arab members of OPEC, affecting the US and other Western powers that had supported Israel. As discussed in Chapter 15, the oil embargo led to lines at gas stations and inflation in the US and other Western economies.

The Yom Kippur War burst the bubble of Israeli military dominance and negatively affected the Israeli economy. When I returned to Israel for a short visit in 1980, the national mood had soured along with the economy, compared to my visit a decade earlier. Recently, Israel was surprised again in October 2023 as Palestinians from Gaza staged a deadly incursion into Israeli settlements across the border.

Many Jews in the diaspora firmly supported Israel in these two conflicts. However, the Jewish population was not monolithic about Israel nor about matters of faith. In the US, there were three major branches of Judaism.

Orthodox Jews strictly followed the traditions established during centuries of Jewish habitation in Eastern Europe. Synagogues were the centre of religious life and needed to be within walking distance from homes (riding on the Sabbath was forbidden). Prayers and ceremonies such as reading portions of the Torah (Old Testament) were strictly in the original Hebrew. No musical accompaniments such as an organ or choir during religious services were permitted. Men and women prayed separately. Men always wore skull caps (yarmulkes), while married women in some communities shaved their hair and wore wigs.

Families kept kosher, avoiding pork and shellfish, as well as separating meat from dairy. Jewish life followed a calendar of holidays starting with the New Year (Rosh Hashanah) and the Day of Atonement (Yom Kippur) in the fall and then proceeding to Passover in the spring. Children attended religious schools where they learned Hebrew and studied the Torah and Talmud, but only boys had a Bar Mitzvah when they reached their 13th birthdays. Rabbis were the ultimate religious and, in some places, civil authorities.

In the US, it is estimated that only 10% of Jews now regard themselves as Orthodox.[14]

Reform Judaism started in Germany in the early 1800s. A small group of rabbis decided that Jewish customs needed to be updated and modernized. They believed that some of the traditional Orthodox beliefs were not appropriate for the modern age. For example, they used local languages instead of Hebrew for synagogue services, which could include organ music and an organized choir. Men and women prayed together, and both boys and girls were confirmed at age 16 in a ceremony marking the completion of their Jewish education and their acceptance of the faith. Kosher dietary laws were eased. Leaders of the Reform movement abandoned customs such as skull caps, prayer shawls and tefillin (phylacteries). Some allowed modification of strict rules preventing any form of work on the Sabbath, such as forbidding turning on electrical switches.

Reform Judaism was brought to the US from Germany under the leadership of Rabbi Isaac Wise. He was the editor of an important American Reform prayer book published in 1857 and was instrumental in establishing Reform institutions [the Union of American Hebrew Congregations (1873), Hebrew Union College (1875) and the Central Conference of American Rabbis (1889)].

These organizations debated use of both English and Hebrew in prayer services, inclusion of certain ceremonies in worship, and support of Zionism to establish a Jewish homeland in what was then known as Palestine.

It is estimated that by The Magical Decade about 40% of American Jews were Reform, making it the largest branch of Judaism in the US.[14]

Besides Orthodox and Reform Judaism, the third major denomination was Conservative Judaism. Conservative Jews believed that biblical and Talmudic rules are subject to interpretation and change over time, but that traditional customs should be maintained. The Conservative movement accepted scientific and historical research rather than the belief that the Bible was literally the Word of God, as held by Orthodox Jews.

Rabbi Zacharias Frankel became the head of the Jewish Theological Seminary in Breslau, Germany, in the mid-1800s when he wrote a series of influential books outlining the basic beliefs of the Conservative Jewish movement.

Conservative Judaism did not have a distinct theology. It was a coalition of beliefs that emphasized the importance of traditions that need to be interpreted for modern times.

In the US, Conservative Judaism's institutions included the United Synagogue of America, the Jewish Theological Seminary and the Rabbinical Assembly. About 18% of American Jews considered themselves as Conservative. Overall, however, Jews comprised only about 2% of the total U.S. population.[14]

Personally, I was raised in a Conservative Jewish family. My father came from an Orthodox Jewish background, while my maternal grandparents were culturally Jewish but not observant. At the age of 13 I had a Bar Mitzvah at a synagogue on the South Side of Chicago (the building is now a Black Baptist Church). I became less observant during The Magical Decade, although I still identified as Jewish, especially after my visit to Israel in 1970. I was not dogmatic about religion, however, as I realized there were many paths of faith.

During The Magical Decade, while a majority of Americans were Protestant Christians, that number was diminishing, so that by 2012 Protestants comprised less than half the US population, according to a Pew Research Survey report.[15] The report stated that among the Americans who were self-professed Christians, 21% of the total population were Catholic and 48% were Protestant. Of the entire U.S. population, according to Pew, 15% were Mainline Protestants, while 25% were Evangelical Protestants, and 7% historically Black Protestants. The mainline Protestant denominations including Presbyterians, Episcopalians and Methodists have been declining in adherents, while others, including Evangelicals and Pentecostals, have grown. This change in demographics began in the early 1960s and accelerated during The Magical Decade. According to data from Gallup, the percentage of Americans who considered themselves Protestants dropped by about 9% during The Magical Decade, falling from about 69% in 1965 to about 60% in 1975.[16]

In contrast, Evangelicalism has increased, although Evangelicals represent a wide range of beliefs ranging from fundamentalism to more liberal interpretations. According to historian David Bebbington, general beliefs among Evangelicals include: 1) conversionism, or the importance of being 'born again'; 2) respect for biblical authority; 3) the centrality of the Crucifixion and Resurrection of Jesus Christ; and 4) religious and social activism. The latter has found expression in mainly conservative politics.[17]

Meanwhile, in 1973 Spencer Kimball became president of the Church of Latter-Day Saints, also known as the Mormons. Up to that time, the Mormons did not allow Blacks to become priests or engage in some rituals. Kimball wrote against segregation but at first supported church doctrine that discriminated against Blacks. In 1978, just after The Magical Decade, Kimball and other Mormon leaders announced they had received a divine revelation allowing Blacks to enter the priesthood and to participate in all Mormon religious ceremonies.

The 1960s also marked the introduction from foreign lands of new forms of spirituality previously absent in the US. Islam was brought to the US from the Middle East and practised primarily by Black Muslims. Temples were established in major American urban areas with large Black populations.

Malcolm X was a Black Muslim religious and civil rights leader who promoted Black empowerment and Islamic beliefs in the Black community. He became the minister at temples of the Nation of Islam, the formal name of the Black Muslim religious movement, in Philadelphia and New York. Malcolm X later became friends with African-American boxer Cassius Clay and influenced him to convert to Islam and join the Nation of Islam. Clay changed his name to Muhammad Ali in February 1964 and then became the boxing heavyweight champion of the world. Malcolm X was assassinated by rivals in February 1965. The previous year Malcolm X's autobiography, written with journalist Alex Haley, was published and describes his spiritual conversion.[18] The book became a perennial bestseller and in 1998 *Time* magazine named it one of the ten most influential nonfiction books.

Other foreign religions such as Buddhism and related practices, such as meditation espoused by Maharishi Mahesh Yogi in India, were also adopted in the US. Adherents followed his tenets of peace, nonviolence and daily meditation. The practice of Transcendental Meditation (TM), a form of mindfulness promoted by the Maharishi, has become mainstream, and the practice of TM has been proven to reduce blood pressure, anxiety and other disorders.

While in college, I took a short extracurricular TM course to learn the technique. I was given a mantra, or word, on which to concentrate while rhythmically breathing with my eyes closed sitting still. I was taught to ignore other sounds and distractions as I focused on repeating my mantra in my thoughts. I found the practice relaxing and soothing and still occasionally meditate.

Another import from Indian tradition during The Magical Decade was the Hare Krishna sect, founded in

1966 by A.C. Bhaktivedanta Swami Prabhupada. Adherents to the Hare Krishna sect wore saffron robes; shaved their heads; ate vegetarian food; avoided tobacco, alcohol and caffeinated drinks; privately used prayer beads to repeat the names of Krishna 108 times; and publicly chanted the Hare Krishna mantra in groups in public places such as airports and shopping malls. I remember seeing them in train and bus stations, and on campus in Ann Arbor.

The movement became popular among young hippies in the West and was publicized by Beatle George Harrison in his song "My Sweet Lord." In recent years, some Asian Indian immigrants who have moved to the West have adopted its rituals and thoughts.

While founded in the 1950s, Scientology is another belief that became publicized during The Magical Decade. Science fiction writer L. Ron Hubbard wrote a book, Dianetics, published in 1950. In 1952, the Church of Scientology, based on the book, was established in Los Angeles. The church claims 5,000 churches throughout the globe and eight million members globally, numbers disputed by critics.[19] Scientology has been variously described as a religion, a business or a cult. It is based on improving oneself by achieving various levels of spiritual advancement. Members undergo interrogations called 'auditing,' during which they are asked about intimate details of their lives. The Church has amassed an estimated $2.5 billion in contributions members give for auditing and other training.[19]

The Church has actively sought celebrities to join as members. Actors Tom Cruise, Kirstie Alley and John Travolta have been long-term adherents of Scientology.

Other actors, such as Nicole Kidman, dabbled in Scientology but later left.

Internationally, the Church of Scientology has been officially labelled as a sect in France, and Russia banned it in 2021. Other nations have declared it a religion and others have not but still have allowed it to operate. In the US, the Church has faced a series of lawsuits claiming harassment of former members, fraud and human trafficking.[19] In general, the Church has won these cases because of arbitration agreements previously signed by members as a condition of joining. Personally, I have been sceptical of Scientology and concerned about the control it allegedly exerts over its members.

While not a formal religion, astrology is a belief that goes back to the Middle Ages that the movement (as seen from Earth) of the Moon and planets affects human behaviour. The Magical Decade marked two major astronomical events. First, the 'Uranus Pluto' conjunction presaged the Summer of Love in San Francisco starting in 1967 when the hippie cultural revolution involving drugs, sex, and rock and roll developed.

According to astrologer Lynn Hayes:

"Much of this was fuelled by the rise of psychedelics thanks to the harmonious sextile from Neptune to the revolutionary duo Uranus and Pluto. Neptune rules the expansion of consciousness, and this consciousness expansion was the theme during much of the 1960s. Consciousness raising was a buzzword that spread from the Black Panthers to the housewives rebelling against the doldrums of their daily life. While Neptune was and will be sextile Pluto between 1948 and 2032, it was in 1966 that Neptune formed that harmonious sextile to Uranus, stimulating the desire to find new ways (Uranus) to find the divine through spirituality, drugs and art (Neptune)."[20]

The second major astrological event of The Magical Decade was the transition from the Age of Pisces to the Age of Aquarius. The Age of Aquarius was believed to be a time of peace, love and understanding. It was celebrated in popular culture, for example, with the song "Age of Aquarius" from the 1969 musical *Hair*. A cover of the song later became a hit by the musical group The 5th Dimension. I heard them perform it live in 1969 at a concert in Crisler Arena at the University of Michigan. I can still hear the chorus in my mind more than 50 years later.

While certainly not believers in astrology, the Apollo 13 crew named their Lunar Module 'Aquarius.' It turned out to be their lifeboat in April 1970 when an explosion in an oxygen tank on the way to the Moon prevented them from landing. Personally, I did not put much stock in astrology and regarded it as superstition. I did not understand how the movements of the Moon and planets could predict human behaviour and future events.

A different set of beliefs involved use of psychedelic drugs, including mushrooms, mescaline and peyote. Author Carlos Castañeda presented them as part of religious rituals to expand consciousness (see Chapter 5).

While it did not claim to be a religion, the practice of 'EST' was popular in the early 1970s among some elites. EST was a part of the Large Group Awareness Training movement that developed during The Magical Decade.[21] Wernher Erhard founded EST in San Francisco in 1971. Participants paid hundreds of dollars to attend weekend seminars to learn how to handle life situations. The seminars were held at fancy hotels and attracted celebrities such as Yoko Ono and actress Valerie Harper. The goal of the seminars was said to be self-actualization.

The EST program consisted of two all-weekend sessions lasting until midnight. The participants were encouraged to admit their faults and mistakes. During the program, they submitted to verbal abuse, motivational speeches, sleep deprivation and hunger. They were encouraged to 'get it,' which was vaguely defined as self-awareness and understanding. I was suspicious about the underlying motivation of EST seminars – was Erhard more interested in the thousands of dollars from seminar admission fees or in personal awareness (or both)?

The Magical Decade led to changes both in established religions and new spiritual practices. These developments included Vatican II reforms in the Catholic faith, the rise of Evangelicals among Protestants, the increase in adherents of Reform Judaism, and decisions about ending racial discrimination among Mormons.

At the same time, there was increased interest in foreign-based religions such as Hinduism and Buddhism, especially among young people. They followed gurus such as Maharishi Mahesh Yogi with his Transcendental Meditation, and A.C. Bhaktivedanta Swami Prabhupada, who founded the Hare Krishna sect.

There were also homegrown quasi-religious movements. Starting in the US, the Church of Scientology became a powerful sect, luring Hollywood stars. Using some similar techniques, EST seminars attracted professionals and celebrities to its meetings. Astrology did not claim to be a religion nor was it an organized movement, but it involved spiritual beliefs that the paths of the planets led to changes in human behaviour and that future events could be predicted.

In general, spirituality became more important in peoples' lives during The Magical Decade, while at the same time strict adherence to mainline religions diminished. As for myself, I maintained my Jewish identity and beliefs but was not that observant.

CHAPTER 4

June 1966: The law and *Miranda*

The US Supreme Court made many important legal rulings during The Magical Decade that have affected my daily life and that of my fellow Americans. The law provides a framework to organize commerce, employment, government and personal relations.

Both of my younger brothers studied law. One, Ken, became a prosecutor seeking justice by putting lawbreakers in jail. The other, Jeff, was a police officer, and later a police chief, trying to keep us safe from the 'bad guys.'

I was intellectually fascinated by the law. Indeed, one of my favourite television series was *The Paper Chase* starring John Houseman as Professor Kingsfield. The series and movie (1973) were based on the 1971 novel about the adventures of a first-year Harvard Law School student learning contract law, trying to survive the imperious Kingsfield, and ending up dating his daughter. While I found the law interesting as a subject, I did not want to 'do law' myself, as I had a more scientific bent.

In 1965, at the beginning of The Magical Decade, the Supreme Court still had a liberal tilt. Earl Warren was appointed Chief Justice by President Dwight D. Eisenhower in 1953. He had been a political conservative while serving as Governor of California, but his rulings became more liberal as he presided as Chief Justice from 1953–1969. Joining him on the liberal side were Associate Justices William O. Douglas, Hugo Black and William Brennan (FIG 4-1). The conservatives on the Court included Felix Frankfurter and John Marshall Harlan.

FIG 4-1: Supreme Court of the US in the mid-1960s.
(Photo credit - Supreme Court)

Four themes dominated the Supreme Court deliberations during the 1960s. The first was race relations. The most important ruling of the first decade of the Warren Court was *Brown v. Board of Education* in 1954. The justices declared unanimously that segregation was unconstitutional. As noted above, they overturned precedents from the 1800s allowing 'separate but equal' accommodations, as decided in *Plessy v. Ferguson* in 1896.

The second trend was to give criminal defendants more rights. Fortunately, I was never arrested, although I came close while covering the May Day anti-war protests in Washington, DC in 1971 (see Chapter 10). Previously in 1963, in *Gideon v. Wainwright*, the Court had declared that states must provide legal counsel at trial to poor defendants who could not afford to pay a lawyer. The court unanimously agreed that to receive a fair trial, legal representation was required. The next year, in 1964, the Court ruled that suspects had a right to legal counsel during police interrogations, as well as during trials. This case, *Escobedo v. Illinois*, was also decided by a 5–4 majority.

In *Miranda v. Arizona*, the Court ruled on 7 June 1966, that criminal suspects undergoing questioning needed to be informed of their right against self-incrimination and their right to consult with an attorney – court-appointed if they could not afford one. It required that suspects understood their rights and had waived them before interrogations began; otherwise, their testimony could not be used at trial.

The text of the 'Miranda warnings' stated: "You have the right to remain silent. Anything you say can and will be used against you in a court of law. You have the right to an attorney. If you cannot afford an attorney, one will be provided for you."[22]

This 5–4 decision by the Supreme Court in 1966 at the beginning of The Magical Decade profoundly changed how US police could question criminal suspects. Giving the defendant these Miranda warnings became an integral part of police procedures.

Police officers found these rulings unduly restrictive but had no choice but to obey them. Actually, many defendants were willing to waive these rights because they wanted an opportunity to tell their own side of the story, according to my brother Jeff, a lawyer and police officer. More educated defendants learned to say nothing to police and refer them to their attorney, but common criminals often agreed to talk.

Another important area in the law that affected criminal suspects was new rulings on search and seizure. In a landmark ruling, *Terry v. Ohio*, the US Supreme Court in 1968 ruled that 'stop and frisk' activities by police were justified when police had a reasonable belief that a crime was to be committed.[23] In this case, a police officer watched three men, including John Terry, checking out a store for a robbery. Because the officer believed a crime was about to be committed, he stopped and frisked Terry, finding a gun. The case, among others decided during The Magical Decade, hinged on the tension between Fourth Amendment protection from unwarranted searches versus the obligation of police to prevent crime.

By an 8–1 vote, the Court held that police could frisk and question suspicious individuals if they have a reasonable cause for stop and frisk. The police can do so, according to the Court, even if they do not have sufficient probable cause to arrest the individual.

Besides search and seizure, rules for obtaining blood from suspects for alcohol levels also came before the Court. In 1966, the question in *Schmerber v. California* was whether drawing a blood sample required a warrant. The Court, in a contentious 5–4 decision, ruled that drawing blood ordinarily did require a warrant, but not in this case because a delay to get a warrant would allow the body to naturally process the alcohol so levels would drop.

A third trend in the law was an expansion of the right to privacy. Although there is no specific mention in the US Constitution of such a right, this right was inferred in a series of cases decided by the Court during The Magical Decade.

In a 7–2 decision in June 1965, the Court struck down a Connecticut law that made contraceptives illegal. The *Griswold v. Connecticut* ruling established a right to marital privacy.[24] The case revolved around an 1879 Connecticut law that banned use of or encouragement to use contraceptives. The majority argued that while the US Constitution did not explicitly grant a right to marital privacy in the Bill of Rights, it can be derived from rights against unwarranted government intrusion as applied to marriages. While *Griswold* legalized contraceptives for married couples, a follow-on case in 1972 extended the right to unmarried couples. In *Eisenstadt v. Baird*, the majority ruled that criminalization of contraceptives by unmarried but not married couples violated the Due Process Clause.

This implied constitutional right of marital privacy was one of the bases for the Court's decision to permit abortion in the landmark June 1973 *Roe v. Wade* case (see Chapter 14).[25] The Court said there were competing interests of the autonomy of the mother to control her body versus the life of a foetus. It initially used a trimester framework, which allowed abortion without restriction during the first trimester, regulations during the second trimester to protect the health of the mother, and restrictions on abortion during the third trimester when the foetus is potentially viable (see Chapter 14 about foetal viability).

Thirty years later in 2022, the Supreme Court reversed itself on *Roe*. In his majority opinion in *Dobbs v. Jackson Women's Health*, Associate Justice Samuel Alito wrote that *Roe* had been wrongly decided and that there was no right to privacy in the Constitution.[26] Critics worried that other rights based on the right to marital privacy are now also in jeopardy. This is especially true of the 5–4 ruling in June 2015 of *Obergefell v. Hodges,* which declared state bans on same-sex marriage unconstitutional under the Due Process and Equal Protection clauses of the Fourteenth Amendment. However, the US Congress in December 2022 passed the Respect for Marriage Act to allay concerns that the Supreme Court could also reverse itself on same sex or interracial marriage. The law required that states recognize marriages legally performed in another state.

A fourth legal trend during The Magical Decade was to loosen obscenity laws restricting sexual expression but to tighten rules against child pornography. The 1957 case *Roth v. United States* led to a new definition of obscenity. In a decision written by Justice William Brennan, obscenity was defined as material whose: "dominant theme taken as a whole appeals to the prurient interest" of the "average person, applying contemporary community standards."[27] This differed from earlier definitions because it uses "dominant theme" as the criteria as opposed to isolated passages, and "average person" rather than susceptible people.

In 1973, the Supreme Court in *Miller v. California* offered an updated, more specific definition of obscenity, which continues to be applied today.[28] The definition was three-pronged:

1. Whether the average person, applying contemporary "community standards," would find that the work, taken as a whole, appeals to the prurient interest;
2. whether the work depicts or describes, in an offensive way, sexual conduct or excretory functions, as specifically defined by the applicable state law: and
3. whether the work, taken as a whole, lacks serious literary, artistic, political, or scientific value.

This definition was formulated before the internet, which by its reach makes it more difficult to determine contemporary community standards.

These mid-century legal decisions are still in the headlines and impact our society today. Under the *stare decisis* doctrine, courts are obliged to follow previously established precedents unless there is an overwhelming reason to make a change. This occurs rarely, but happened, for example, in 1954 with *Brown v. Board of Education* making segregation unconstitutional. In more recent times, *Roe v. Wade* was also overturned, sending decisions on abortion to the states.

Abortion, pornography, voting rights, search and seizure, race relations and many more – the legal issues decided during The Magical Decade continue to prompt scrutiny half a century later. These decisions affect the everyday lives of millions of Americans, including me. They set the 'rules of the road' for our behaviour.

CHAPTER 5

June 1967:
Drugs

I attended a suburban high school from 1965–1968 (my freshman year in 1964 was in Chicago before our family moved). It was in a conservative area, where drugs did not seem to me to be very prevalent at the time. It was not until I started at the University of Michigan in Ann Arbor in 1968 that I came face-to-face with the drug revolution.

Popularization of drugs by rock stars ignited interest in marijuana, LSD and other drugs at the start of The Magical Decade. As noted in Chapter 1, The Beatles started using marijuana after getting high with Bob Dylan on their 1964 trip to the US. They reportedly tried LSD the next year in London and Beverly Hills. The Beatles graduated to stronger drugs, with Paul McCartney allegedly snorting cocaine in 1967 and John Lennon reportedly using inhaled heroin in 1969, according to later news reports.[29]

Drug use was common in the late 1960s among many rock stars. However, it exacted a heavy toll. Jimi Hendrix,

Brian Jones, Janis Joplin and Jim Morrison, among others, died early probably due to a drug-filled lifestyle.

At the same time, Harvard psychology professors Timothy O'Leary and Richard Alpert were promoting use of LSD as a means to alter consciousness. "Turn on, tune in and drop out" was the phrase O'Leary developed in 1966.[30] On the West Coast, Ken Kesey, author of *One Flew Over the Cuckoo's Nest*, began to hold happenings fuelled by LSD called 'acid tests.' Those attending became known as the 'Merry Pranksters,' and included artists and musicians such as the Grateful Dead. Novelist Tom Wolfe celebrated Kesey and the Merry Pranksters in his 1969 book, *The Electric Kool-Aid Acid Test*.

At the same time, anthropologist Carlos Castañeda, who was born in Peru, popularized use of psychedelic 'magic' mushrooms, peyote, mescaline and psilocybin in a series of books starting with *The Teachings of Don Juan: A Yaqui Way of Knowledge*, published in 1968.[31] While presented as nonfiction teachings of a Yaqui shaman, critics have claimed Castañeda's works were actually fiction. Whether true or not, Castañeda introduced a wider audience to the use of mushrooms and related substances to alter consciousness.

Drug exploration exploded during the 1967 'Summer of Love' in San Francisco. Up to 100,000 people were drawn by drugs, music, free and open sex, and anti-war activism to the Haight-Ashbury district of the city.[32] The festival-like atmosphere marked the high point of the hippie movement. Marijuana, known as 'weed,' and psychedelics such as LSD were ubiquitous. Drug use was celebrated in the music of the time by Jefferson Airplane, The Who, Jimi Hendrix and The Doors, among many other musical groups.

The next summer, in 1968, I arrived in Ann Arbor as a naïve freshman with no drug experience. I quickly became introduced to marijuana, taking tokes (puffs) of weed as joints (marijuana cigarettes) were passed around at parties. I did not tolerate alcohol very well, getting drunk with just a few drinks. I did not know my limits when I arrived. I ended up at my first freshmen dorm party sitting drunk on a toilet seat, vomiting between my legs. It was not pretty. With alcohol I would fall asleep quickly and miss the party. I became a moderate drinker as I learned my limitations, but I was definitely a lightweight.

In contrast, with marijuana I would get a nice high that allowed me to continue partying. Yes, I did inhale. However, I was acutely aware at that time that selling, buying or even possessing marijuana was illegal. I realized that a drug conviction would be detrimental to my goal of going into medicine, so I never had my own stash (supply). It would take half a century for medical and recreational use of marijuana to become legal in many, but not all, states. Being busted (arrested) was all too common for Blacks and people of colour, while White offenders often did not face serious consequences.

I was offered LSD on several occasions in 1968 and thereafter, but I was frightened by the possibility of a 'bad trip.' I had heard of hallucinations, paranoia, mental breakdowns, injuries and even rare suicides from LSD. Mainly, I demurred from using LSD because I did not want to lose self-control. I also did not use cocaine (popular in the late 1970s), heroin, or MDMA, better known as 'ecstasy' or 'molly,' for similar reasons.

I did try hashish, a more potent form of marijuana derived from a resin produced by the flowers of the marijuana plant (trichomes). One memorable experience was smoking hash in a tent in suburban Washington, DC while covering the March on Washington in 1969 for *The Michigan Daily*. The party was in the backyard of the home of a *Daily* staffer whose father was employed by the federal government. He was understandably concerned about having a bunch of high college students smoking hash in his backyard. I remember getting very high in the smoky tent as we giggled recounting the anti-war events of the day (see Chapter 10).

After entering medical school in 1972, my concerns about a drug conviction, even for marijuana, heightened, so my minimal usage declined even further. This did not stop some of my classmates who got high on a regular basis, although generally not while working at a hospital or clinic.

At the start of The Magical Decade back in 1965, my impression was that illicit drug use was uncommon and usually confined to pockets on the East and West Coasts. Prompted by rebellion against the status quo, the hippie movement, rock music groups and left-wing anti-war political movements, these influences each promoted drug use for various reasons.

The mantra of 'drugs, sex and rock 'n' roll became a way of living for some in this counterculture. The 'Summer of Love' in the San Francisco Bay area in 1967 and anti-Vietnam War events in Washington DC in 1969–1972 were gatherings of tens of thousands of young people who exchanged experiences and brought this culture back to their local areas.

By the end of The Magical Decade in 1975, marijuana was firmly established among young people as a means to get high and became a staple at parties, musical happenings and political events. Although technically illegal, police enforcement was spotty and, as noted, Black and brown urban communities faced more legal jeopardy from weed than White suburban kids. I smoked weed at gatherings but did not buy marijuana nor possess it. I have not used marijuana since I smoked a joint with my son and his college roommate in their fraternity house over 15 years ago.

LSD had lost its lustre except among fringe groups due to the risks of bad trips. The possibility of disorientation, hallucinations and suicidal thoughts were a disincentive to LSD use. Although generally less severe, the same types of side effects from magic mushrooms containing psilocybin also limited their general use.

Cocaine became increasingly popular during the late 1970s. Entertainers and businesspeople used it to get bursts of energy. It was very addictive and expensive so that people who used it regularly ended up in a downward life spiral – losing their jobs, developing physical dependence and entering poverty.

The drug culture subsequently faded in popularity, with the exception of marijuana. Marijuana has now become legal for both medical and recreational use in many states, including Illinois. It is an important source of revenue, as it is highly taxed in those states. There are some state efforts to pardon or expunge the records of those who were arrested and convicted of marijuana use during The Magical Decade. Marijuana still remains a prohibited substance under federal regulations despite legalization by certain states. The US Drug Enforcement Administration lists it as a Schedule 1 drug, for which there is "no currently accepted medical use and a high potential for abuse." However, the 'Feds' generally do not prosecute individuals for marijuana possession, leaving the matter to the states.

The Magical Decade marked an exponential increase in the use of drugs in the US and around the world. This was especially true for young people, such as me, in their teens and 20s, but also those younger and older. Now marijuana has been legalized, but controversies over drug use continue half a century later. An ongoing serious problem remains with abuse of prescription drugs and resulting drug overdoses, especially from fentanyl and crystal meth.

CHAPTER 6

December 1967: Medical advances

"When you come to a fork in the road, take it!"[33]

These sage words of advice from legendary New York Yankee baseball catcher Yogi Berra applied to me in 1971, midway through The Magical Decade. At that point I was prepared for a career in either medicine or journalism, and I needed to decide which fork to travel.

I had been an editor of my high school newspaper and was a reporter, and eventually managing editor, of *The Michigan Daily.* In addition, I had a summer internship in 1970 on the copy desk of *The Cleveland Press.* I was well-trained in journalism, even though the University of Michigan did not have a formal journalism degree (*The Daily* was on-the-job training.). Many of my friends and peers planned to become journalists and had started applying for positions.

At the same time, I was also pre-med, majoring in zoology, and taking the requisite courses for medical school, including the hated organic chemistry. I had good grades and test scores. My father was a physician and he pointed out that medicine was a more stable source of income than journalism, where only the top people made money and the vast majority were at the bottom end of professional pay scales.

Another consideration was that physicians still could write, while it was rare for writers to become physicians. After a lot of soul searching, I decided in 1971 to go the medicine route, but I promised myself I would continue writing. I was accepted by three medical schools and decided to stay in Ann Arbor.

During my time at the University of Michigan Medical School, 1972–1976, I witnessed several major advances in medicine.

Organ transplantation comprised the first revolutionary advance. The 'father' of organ transplantation was Dr Thomas Starzl. He developed an interest in liver biology as a young surgeon. Starzl did research with animals, and in 1963 tried the first human liver transplant, which was unsuccessful. Much of his early work was at the University of Colorado Health Center, although he later moved to the University of Pittsburgh.

Starzl then pioneered organ preservation, surgical transplantation techniques and control of infection and coagulation, issues that were all roadblocks to successful surgery. He investigated immune suppression to prevent organ rejection, and after The Magical Decade, played a key role in the development of potent immunosuppressant drugs, including cyclosporine and tacrolimus. In 1967, Starzl successfully resumed liver transplantation and was at the forefront of the technique internationally. He was also actively involved in kidney, whole pancreas and pancreatic islet transplants.

Also in December 1967, Dr Christiaan Barnard performed the first human-to-human heart transplant at Groote-Schuur Hospital in Cape Town, South Africa. He transplanted the heart of an accident victim into 54-year-old Louis Washkansky. Washkansky lived for only 18 days but regained consciousness. He died of pneumonia due to immunosuppressant drugs. This first heart transplant received worldwide media attention. Barnard went on to do a second transplant in January 1968. The recipient, Philip Blaiberg, survived for 19 months. An estimated 100 heart transplants were attempted worldwide in 1968, but the high mortality rate soon dampened enthusiasm. However, improvements in immunosuppressive regimens, treatment of infections, coagulation control, and heart procurement and preservation techniques led to a resumption of heart transplantation.

In the United States, Dr Michael DeBakey was a pioneering cardiovascular surgeon who first developed Dacron blood vessel grafts, repairs of aortic aneurysms, coronary artery bypass grafts, carotid endarterectomies, and ventricular assist devices. He worked at Baylor University School of Medicine, becoming the chairman of surgery, president, and eventually chancellor over a long and distinguished medical career. While his rival, Dr Denton Cooley, performed the first American heart transplant in 1968, DeBakey did the first multiple organ transplant that same year. He removed a heart, liver and two kidneys from an accident victim and transplanted them into four different individuals.

As a medical student at the University of Michigan 1972–1976, I was an eyewitness to some of these advances.

For example, I saw some of the earliest heart-lung machines. Dr Herbert Sloan at Michigan was responsible for improved heart-lung machines, including the type used by Dr Barnard for the first heart transplant. The first heart transplant at U-M was unsuccessfully attempted in 1968; a formal cardiac transplantation program did not begin until 1984. Since then, there have been 800 heart transplants in Ann Arbor and an even greater number of ventricular assist device placements.

Besides transplantation, another great medical advance I witnessed during The Magical Decade was the introduction of Computerized Tomography (CT) scanning. This was of special interest to me because my father was a radiologist for whom traditional X-ray imaging was the basis of his profession. While X-rays were good to see abnormalities such as bone fractures, they were not able to visualize the brain, many organs or soft tissues.

The first experimental CT scan was developed in the United Kingdom by Godfrey Hounsfield in 1968 at a research branch of EMI, the company that also had The Beatles as clients.[34] The early developments were aimed at brain imaging, for which there was a great need since plain X-rays were not useful. CT scanning was first used in clinical practice in October 1971. Hounsfield and EMI produced the first commercial CT scanner in 1972. Hounsfield received a knighthood and the Nobel Prize in Medicine in 1979 for his efforts. (Dr Allen McCormick of Tufts University shared the Nobel Prize.) In 1974, Dr Robert Ledley, a professor at Georgetown University, developed the first whole-body CT scanner.

CT scanning quickly became used worldwide. It was the modality of choice to visualize the brain and was also used for more detailed imaging of the lungs, abdomen, paranasal sinuses and other soft tissues. It is estimated that by 1980, more than 3 million CT scans had been performed worldwide.[35]

The first CT scanners arrived at the University of Michigan in the mid-1970s at the end of The Magical Decade, as I was graduating from medical school. I was astounded at the detail that CT scanning had brought. I could see all the structures of the brain inside the skull for the first time through noninvasive visualization. Other soft tissues such as the lungs, liver and pancreas, as well as the paranasal sinuses, were also easily seen using CT scanning. Within a short time, CT scans had a profound effect on patient diagnosis and treatment. They also revolutionized traditional medical imaging, which had relied on plain X-rays (which my radiologist father had interpreted).

A third paradigm shift in medicine during The Magical Decade in which I participated was a more detailed understanding of the physiology of the immune system. While the existence of antibodies against foreign pathogens had been known for decades, the process by which natural infection or vaccination elicited these antibodies was unknown.

Immunologist Jacques Miller was born in France but did his research studies initially in England. He discovered in the 1960s that the thymus, once thought to be just a vestigial organ, played a key role in the immune response. Experimental animals without a thymus could not fight some infections, especially viral ones, and were unable to reject foreign tissues.

Miller moved to Australia in 1966, where he headed a lab at the Walter and Eliza Hall Institute of Medical

Research in Melbourne. Miller made the pioneering discovery there that there are two types of the white blood cells called lymphocytes.[36] B, or bone-marrow-derived, lymphocytes develop into plasma cells that synthesize protective antibodies. T, or thymus-derived, lymphocytes are responsible for graft rejection, anti-tumour activity, protection against viral and other intracellular infections, and other functions of cellular immunity.

While Miller did primarily animal research, physicians such as Dr Robert Good learned from patients with inherited inborn errors of immunity. Working at the University of Minnesota, Good demonstrated the importance of the thymus gland in humans and described a new syndrome, later named after him, of thymoma with agammaglobulinemia (thymic tumour with a lack of antibodies).

In 1968, he performed the first successful human-to-human bone marrow transplant. The patient was a five-month-old infant with severe combined immunodeficiency (SCID), who was saved from death by infection with a bone marrow transplant from his sister. Another patient with SCID came to be known as the 'bubble boy' and survived for a while in isolation, but efforts to reconstitute his immune system eventually failed. Good took advantage of these 'experiments of nature' in patients to better understand human immunology.

During The Magical Decade from 1972–1982, Good was president of the Sloan-Kettering Cancer Institute in New York. He also trained a whole cadre of specialists in human immunology. His fellows included several pioneering human immunologists with whom I later worked. His *New York Times* obituary in 2003 called Good "the founder of modern immunology."[37]

Just after The Magical Decade, Dr Richard Hong was a mentor of mine during my internship and residency in paediatrics at the University of Wisconsin, Madison from 1976–1979. He was actively engaged in research, transplanting thymic tissue into immunodeficient human patients. An outstanding clinician and researcher, Dr Hong, who trained under Dr Good, was a role model for me.

Then from 1979–1982, just after The Magical Decade, I undertook a fellowship in immunology in the Department of Paediatrics at the University of California, San Francisco. Dr Arthur Ammann, who had also trained with Good, was the head of the program.[38] When I arrived, the research focus was on the use of foetal thymus transplants to correct inborn errors of immunity.

During the last part of my fellowship in San Francisco, we took care of the first paediatric AIDS patients. I drew blood (without gloves) on an immunodeficient infant born to a woman who was a prostitute and drug addict. The virus had not been identified, and we did not take precautions while caring for the infant on the paediatric ward. The child was one of the first cases of proven maternal-foetal transmission of human immunodeficiency virus (HIV), which was just being characterized. As soon as a blood test was available to detect HIV infection, I took one and had a negative test, to my relief.

Dr Ammann went on to play an important role in describing paediatric AIDS, warning about transmissibility in blood products, and leading a worldwide effort against HIV infection, especially in children. His associate, Dr Diane Wara, was an outstanding clinician who was an advocate for women in medicine and particularly in research.

Dr Morton Cowan was the third member of the team, who specialized in paediatric bone marrow transplantation to treat malignancies and immunodeficiencies.

After my fellowship, I returned to Chicago in 1982 to an academic faculty position at Rush University Medical Center, where I was an assistant professor of immunology, microbiology and paediatrics under Dr Henry Gewurz. This is not the time nor place to describe what happened, but suffice it to say I decided academic medicine was not for me. In July 1987, I joined a private practice of allergy/immunology founded by Dr Salmon Goldberg in 1973 with offices in the Chicago suburbs.

The advancements in medicine during The Magical Decade greatly influenced my later medical career. For example, allergy is the result of an overactive immune system; an understanding of basic immunology is essential to allergy diagnosis and treatment. Also, sinusitis is a common comorbidity of allergy and CT scanning is the gold standard for diagnosis of sinus disease.

I continued part-time at Rush until 1991, doing some teaching and research. In all, I was the author or coauthor of 29 medical publications from 1981–1994. The subject matters of my research included host defences against the pneumococcus bacteria, immunology of sickle cell disease, and characterization of autoimmune diseases in children.

During the preceding years in The Magical Decade, I was able to witness profound changes in medicine, especially with organ transplantation, CT scanning with advanced imaging, and a detailed understanding of the immune system and its inborn errors. It was an exciting time to be in medical school (1972–1976), as medicine advanced at a rapid rate.

CHAPTER 7

January 1969: Politics – two presidents and a war

Inauguration Day, 20 January 1969, was cool and grey, with a noon-time temperature of 35°F. Rain and sleet would arrive later. The day marked the passage of power from retiring President Lyndon B. Johnson to newly elected President Richard M. Nixon. The politics of The Magical Decade were dominated by these two towering presidents – Johnson from 1963–1968 and Nixon from 1969–1974. Both were complicated and controversial men who were torn down politically by their own personality flaws and the Vietnam War.

I personally never met Nixon, but I encountered Johnson twice. The first time was on 16 July 1969, when he attended in person the Apollo 11 Moon launch. Dressed in a dark blue suit, despite the warm humid Florida weather, he and his wife, Lady Bird, watched the Saturn V liftoff carrying Neil Armstrong, Buzz Aldrin and Mike Collins to the Moon. They were escorted by Secret Service guards to sit in the VIP grandstands at the Kennedy Space Center. As a 19 year-old college reporter,

I was situated on the grass in front of the grandstands. I took pictures of the former president as he stood up to acknowledge the applause of the friendly crowd. (FIG 7-1). He appeared sun-tanned and healthy.

FIG 7-1: President Lyndon Johnson at the launch of Apollo 11 on 16 July 1969.
(Photo credit - David Chudwin)

Three years later, I again encountered the former president walking into the Chicago Hilton Hotel with a retinue of Secret Service agents. In the interim, Johnson had had a series of heart attacks. He appeared sallow and tired as he entered. He died of complications from heart disease on 22 January 1973, at age 64 at his ranch in his beloved State of Texas. It was the demise of a man who was at the centre of US politics in the 1950s as senate majority leader, the 1960s as vice president, and then as the 36th President of the United States.

Lyndon Baines Johnson had been sworn into office for his only full four-year term as president on 20 January 1965, right at the beginning of The Magical Decade. His previous inauguration had been tragic. He was in Dallas as vice president with President John F. Kennedy when Kennedy was fatally shot on 22 November 1963. Johnson was hurriedly sworn in on Air Force One, parked at Dallas' Love Field, by Judge Sarah Hughes with his wife, Lady Bird, and Jacqueline Kennedy, in her blood-stained dress, at his side.

I was 13 years old at the time of the Kennedy assassination and was deeply shocked by the murder of the popular young president. It had been 62 years since President William McKinley had been shot and Kennedy's death was completely unexpected. I watched the CBS News coverage in my eighth-grade classroom, one of the only ones in the school building that had a black-and-white television. Walter Cronkite was on the air in white shirt sleeves without his usual jacket. There was a lot of confusion at first, but finally a bulletin from Parkland Hospital stated that Kennedy had died. There were gasps in the classroom and some of the girls started weeping.

The next days were filled with sounds of horse steps on cobblestones, drum cadences, 21-gun salutes, and "Hail to the Chief" as Kennedy's body was returned to Washington, DC. His body, in a flag-draped coffin, lay in state in the Capitol, and he was laid to rest at Arlington National Cemetery on 25 November 1963.

Johnson assumed Kennedy's mantle both as president but also as the guardian of many of his programs. This inherited agenda would lead to both triumphs and tragedies. The new president was faced with important issues, such as race relations, at a time when segregation was finally illegal but still practised. Poverty remained a chronic problem, especially in inner cities and Appalachia. The United States was still behind the Soviets in the Space Race, the Russians having set one record after another. Most significantly, Johnson inherited a simmering but still low-level conflict in Vietnam, where there were 23,000 US forces in 1964.

When he was sworn in for the second time on that January day in 1965, Johnson was still highly popular. He had won the 3 November 1964, election against Senator Barry Goldwater by a landslide, with 61% of the popular vote. (FIG 7-2). I was 14 at the time. While I was too young to vote, I supported Johnson because I thought he was most likely to keep the US at peace and out of war. I passed out leaflets and bumper stickers supporting Johnson in my Chicago neighbourhood ("LBJ for the USA") and campaigned for Johnson along with my good friend Mike Froman (FIG 7-3). We were bipartisan, however, and also supported moderate Republican Charles Percy for the Senate.

FIG 7-2: Campaign buttons from the 1964 election between Lyndon Johnson and Barry Goldwater from the collection of David Chudwin. (Photo credit - David Chudwin)

FIG 7-3: The author *(left)* and his friend Michael Froman on Election Day in November 1964. (Photo credit - David Chudwin)

Johnson was, in many ways, larger than life. At 6 foot 3 inches tall, he was the second-tallest US President (Lincoln beat him out by an inch). He had slicked-back hair, long arms to envelop people in an embrace, and large hands. He was known to be a great persuader, using charm, promises and threats to coerce and cajole people to his point of view. However, he was not a particularly good public speaker on television; his delivery was slow and wooden.

In the US Senate, he rose to the rank of Majority Leader after the 1954 elections and used his power to help his constituents in Texas with appropriations, programs and jobs. Johnson was also chairman of the Senate Space Committee and became the 'godfather' of the US space program. It was no coincidence that the new Manned Spacecraft Center was located in Texas outside of Houston, where construction began in 1962. (It was later named in his honour.)

The year 1965, at the start of The Magical Decade, when I was turning 15, was an important time in Johnson's presidency. In a May 1964 commencement speech at the University of Michigan (where I would later go to college), Johnson had laid out the principles of racial justice and eliminating poverty that he called the "Great Society." In 1965, he pushed through Congress landmark legislation to attempt to accomplish these goals. These important 1965 laws included the Voting Rights Act, Housing and Urban Development Act, Medicare Act, Elementary and Secondary Education Act, and Higher Education Act. They affected virtually all important aspects of American life – education, housing, medical care and elections.

However, 1965 also marked the escalation of US involvement in Vietnam. The Southeast Asian nation had been a French colony but became independent in 1954 after Hồ Chí Minh, a communist, waged a guerilla war with his Viet Minh troops against the colonial French rulers. The northern half of Vietnam went to the communists, while the southern half was proclaimed the Republic of Vietnam in 1955. South Vietnam was led by Ngô Đình Diệm until he was killed in a military coup in 1963. Nguyễn Văn Thiệu was president from 1965 until the eventual fall of the South to North Vietnamese forces in 1975.

Neither regime, based in Hanoi for the North and in Saigon for the South, was democratic. The North was a brutal communist dictatorship. The Diệm regime in the South was a corrupt autocratic regime. However, because it was noncommunist, it was embraced by the US and its allies. The North sought to reunify Vietnam under communist rule and it organized a second guerilla war to 'liberate' South Vietnam. The Viet Cong was its military wing and the National Liberation Front was its political organization.

US involvement in Vietnam began on a small scale in November 1955, when President Dwight D. Eisenhower sent a few US advisers to help train the South Vietnamese army. This was in the middle of the Cold War, and it was US policy to 'contain' communism by aiding regimes which were anticommunist.

In May 1961, President Kennedy sent an additional 400 Special Forces to South Vietnam. US troop strength there increased to about 16,000 US troops under Kennedy's direction by the time he was assassinated in November 1963. That same month, there was the military coup that deposed Diệm; the coup had the tacit approval of the US.

The conflict in Vietnam against communism was one of the hallmarks of Kennedy's activist foreign policy. However, there is some evidence from reporting I did that Kennedy had doubts about the effort. I interviewed anti-war Senator Wayne Morse (D-Oregon) in 1968 for *The Michigan Daily*. Morse stated that Kennedy told him just before his assassination that Kennedy planned to start withdrawing US troops from Vietnam after the 1964 election.[39] For political reasons, Kennedy wanted to wait until after the election, but he was assassinated before then.

Carrying out Kennedy's public plans, Johnson escalated the war by sending increasing numbers of young Americans to Southeast Asia. By 1968, the last year of his presidency, there were over half a million US soldiers in Vietnam. At the same time, casualties mounted. There were 1,928 deaths of US servicemen during 1965 but this rose to 16,899 in 1968.[40]

As a teenager, I had supported Johnson in 1964 as a more peaceful alternative to Senator Barry Goldwater. However, as the troop level and casualties soared, I became disillusioned with Johnson and his policies. His unctuous television speeches on the subject did not help maintain support for, or loyalty to, LBJ.

As casualties rose, this disaffection for Johnson and the Vietnam War became more widespread around the country. Protests started to break out in 1965 with a March teach-in against the war at the University of Michigan. (Students and faculty at the Ann Arbor campus had a long history of political activism.) The protests sprang up on many other campuses with increasing numbers of participants and intensity. I was opposed to the Vietnam War for many reasons (See Chapter 10). I observed and reported on many of these demonstrations, and participated in a few, over the next decade.

Support in the US for the Vietnam War eroded, especially after the Tet Offensive, when on 30 January 1968, Viet Cong soldiers simultaneously attacked 13 cities in South Vietnam. This campaign showed that despite years of war and bombings, the Viet Cong had the momentum to mount a complex military campaign. The Tet Offensive was designed to demoralize South Vietnamese forces, capture territory, even if only temporarily, and send a political message to the American public. Despite taking heavy losses, the Viet Cong accomplished their goals.

In mid-February 1968, CBS News anchorman Walter Cronkite went to Vietnam. On his return, he wrote an editorial that aired on a CBS television special. He wrote in part:

"To say that we are closer to victory today is to believe, in the face of the evidence, the optimists who have been wrong in the past. To suggest we are on the edge of defeat is to yield to unreasonable pessimism. To say that we are mired in stalemate seems the only realistic, yet unsatisfactory conclusion."[41]

When the authoritative newsman called the war a "stalemate," Johnson was later reported to have said that if he had lost Cronkite, he had lost Middle America.

Meanwhile, political forces were afoot in the Democratic Party to deny Johnson another term because of the war. An anti-war senator from Minnesota, Eugene McCarthy, decided to challenge the incumbent president for the Democratic nomination when no one else would take that politically risky step. He scored an unexpectedly strong second place in the 12 March 1968, New Hampshire primary, losing to Johnson by just seven points.

This impressive showing against an incumbent president changed the political landscape. On 16 March, four days later, Senator Robert F. Kennedy, younger brother of the slain president, entered the race against Johnson. With two committed rivals, a weary President Johnson announced on 31 March that: "I will not seek, nor will I accept, the nomination of my party for another term as your president."[42] I watched that live television broadcast; the surprise announcement stunned me and the country.

I was 17 years old and a high school senior at the time. I admired McCarthy's political courage in opposing Johnson when no one else would. As both a poet and a politician, he seemed perhaps too intellectual to be effective, but he had risen in the rough and tumble politics of the Minnesota Democratic Farmer Labor Party. I decided to volunteer in McCarthy's local Illinois campaign (FIG 7-4). I went canvassing on his behalf in nearby Indiana. I also attended Illinois campaign events and even organized a pro-McCarthy student group at my high school. I held a fundraising barbeque at my house, which was attended by over 100 people and had coverage in the local newspaper.

At the time, I was not a supporter of Robert Kennedy because of his earlier 'enforcer' reputation as US Attorney General during his brother's administration. He was a tough political in-fighter who protected his brother's interests and went after his opponents. I did not understand at the time that politicians can learn and grow, as he did. His assassination on 5 June 1968, while I was watching television coverage of his victory in the California primary, came as a complete shock. For the Kennedy family to lose two brothers by assassination was unthinkable. Robert Kennedy's death, and especially that of Martin Luther King, Jr. in Memphis on 4 April 1968, provoked sadness, anger and even rage, leading to riots in major cities.

Meanwhile, McCarthy continued his quixotic quest for the Democratic nomination (FIG 7-4). His campaign asked for volunteers for the Democratic National Convention (DNC) to be held in August in my hometown of Chicago. However, I had to leave that week to start my college career in Ann Arbor at the University of Michigan, which had a trimester system beginning earlier compared to traditional college calendars.

FIG 7-4: Campaign literature from 1968 from the campaigns of Eugene McCarthy, Robert Kennedy and Richard Nixon from the collection of David Chudwin. (Photo credit - David Chudwin)

It was probably a good thing I had left for Ann Arbor, or I would have been in the middle of the Chicago 'police riot' on 28 August 1968, outside the DNC meeting. The McCarthy campaign offices were attacked by the police. Campaign workers and volunteers were beaten up and arrested, including some I knew. As a result, there was a great deal of hostility toward the police (called 'pigs' by protestors at the time) and Chicago Mayor Richard J. Daley.

As I moved into my freshmen dormitory, Alice Lloyd Hall, the chaotic DNC, nominated Vice President Hubert Humphrey as their candidate for president and Senator Walter Mondale of Minnesota as their vice-presidential candidate. I had encountered Humphrey in Chicago in 1965 at the student reception for Gemini 4 astronauts Jim McDivitt and Ed White.

The Republicans had nominated former Vice President Richard M. Nixon for president and Maryland

Governor Spiro T. Agnew for vice president at a convention in Miami three weeks before. I never met Nixon but was wary of him due to his reputation as 'Tricky Dick' for his political dirty tricks.

Nixon grew up and attended college in Southern California. He returned there to practise law after graduating from Duke University Law School in 1937. After working in Washington, DC during World War II, Nixon was elected to the US House of Representatives from California in 1946 and to the US Senate in 1950. There he gained a reputation as a virulent anticommunist. General Dwight Eisenhower selected Nixon to be his running mate in 1952 when Nixon was only 40 years old. Nixon served as vice president during Eisenhower's two terms. Eisenhower gave him more responsibilities than previous vice presidents, and Nixon presided over Cabinet meetings when Eisenhower was ill with a heart attack.

The 1960 presidential election between Nixon and Massachusetts Senator John F. Kennedy was hard fought. Television played a new and important role; a broadcast debate between the two was disastrous for Nixon. He was tired, looked pale and had a five o'clock beard shadow because he declined adequate television face makeup. In contrast, Kennedy was tanned, rested and had expert makeup. Issues in the debate included the economy and US standing versus the Soviet Union in the Cold War. Kennedy's Roman Catholic religion was a thorn for some voters, but he was able to settle their reservations. In the end, Kennedy won a very narrow victory in 1960 in the closest US presidential election in decades.

Nixon was bitter about his loss but decided to run for Governor of California two years later in 1962. His subsequent defeat then led many to write off his political career. After the election, he famously blamed the press and told a news conference, "You won't have Nixon to kick around anymore because, gentlemen, this is my last press conference."[43]

Nixon had a complex personality. He was a loner who had few close friends and kept his inner thoughts to himself. He could be a vicious political infighter who would stoop to illegal tactics; indeed, it was the political 'dirty tricks' and cover-up involved in the Watergate scandal that led to his resignation in 1974. He believed in and tried to portray a 'tough guy' persona, yet was insecure, even to the point of mild paranoia. In times of trouble, he felt sorry for himself and also used alcohol to excess.

According to Nixon biographer Richard Reeves:

"He assumed the worst in people, and he brought out the worst in them ... He clung to the idea of being 'tough.' He thought that was what had brought him to the edge of greatness. But that was what betrayed him. He could not open himself to other men and he could not open himself to greatness."[44]

After his 1968 election, Nixon as president turned his attention to the Vietnam War. Along with Secretary of State Henry Kissinger and Secretary of Defense Melvin Laird, he developed a three-pronged strategy to reduce US involvement. First, the US would train and equip South Vietnamese forces so they could assume the primary combat goals. Second, the US would expand the bombing campaign to include North Vietnam, Laos and Cambodia to put pressure on the communists to come to the bargaining table. The US would also try to convince the North Vietnamese that Nixon was a 'madman' who would resort to nuclear weapons to end the conflict. Finally, the US would promote a diplomatic process with negotiations in Paris with the North Vietnamese to resolve the war.

None of these strategies worked very well. As US forces were withdrawn, the South Vietnamese troops proved incapable of standing up to their communist countrymen. The Tet Offensive in January 1968 showed that the North Vietnamese were able to wage a coordinated campaign against five major cities and other locales all at the same time, even with the presence of US forces.

By the 1972 election year, the number of US military personnel in Vietnam had dropped to 49,000 from over half a million. Yet had it not been for the US Air Force and these remaining American ground troops, the North Vietnamese would have taken over the country in a March 1972 offensive that led to the temporary capture of Quang Tri city by the communists. In the end, US air power proved decisive in 1972, compensating for the mixed performance of South Vietnamese troops.

The bombing campaign was controversial at the time for several reasons. Opponents of the war pointed to civilian casualties, so-called 'collateral damage,' caused by the bombing. They also noted that the covert bombing of Cambodia and Laos helped bring those two ostensibly neutral nations into the fray. Supporters of the war were critical of limitations placed by civilian officials on more extensive bombing, which prevented the Air Force and Navy from attacking the North's key ports, such as Haiphong Harbor, as well as dams, power plants, and some industrial sites for fear of striking Russian or Chinese ships or causing additional Russian or Chinese casualties.

Nuclear bombs were off-limits, but US policy makers sought to create doubts in the minds of the North Vietnamese and their Russian and Chinese allies by creating a narrative that Nixon was reckless and would go nuclear if they did not negotiate. Nixon told his national security adviser, Henry Kissinger, to let the North Vietnamese know he was 'crazy' and willing to use nuclear weapons. He told his chief of staff, Bob Haldeman, that his secret strategy to end the war was to threaten to utilize nukes.

Nixon had hoped for a negotiated settlement, but talks in Paris dragged on for years. The talks began in 1968 and it took until 27 January 1973 for the final accords to be signed by negotiators, Henry Kissinger for the US and Lê Đức Thọ for the North Vietnamese. The provisions of the agreement for a ceasefire were broken almost immediately by both sides, and by March 1973, full-scale fighting had broken out again.

In the meantime, the Watergate scandal intervened in the Nixon presidency. The Watergate complex, built in 1965, was a mixed-use development with offices, apartments and a hotel. The headquarters of the Democratic National Committee (DNC) were located in the offices there.

On 17 June 1972, Washington, DC police arrested five men at the Watergate who were caught red-handed burglarizing the DNC offices. Four of the men were ex-CIA operatives while the fifth, James McCord, was the security chief of Nixon's reelection committee. FBI investigators found that the men reported to White House staffer and former CIA officer E. Howard Hunt and to G. Gordon Liddy, counsel to the reelection committee.

The White House denied any involvement in the break-in, claiming that it was a rogue operation. Investigations by the FBI and *The Washington Post*, guided by a secret source nicknamed 'Deep Throat,' found otherwise. (Associate FBI Director Mark Felt, before he died in 2008, admitted that he had been Deep Throat.) The White House resisted congressional inquiries and covertly attempted to cover up the connection between the burglars and the Nixon reelection committee.

The Senate held televised hearings starting in May 1973 that revealed the existence of a secret White House taping system, which Nixon fought to keep confidential under the guise of executive privilege. The US Supreme Court unanimously ruled on 24 July 1974 that Nixon had to give up the tapes, which proved the existence of a cover-up.

The Judiciary Committee of the US House of Representatives drew up articles of impeachment, but before the full House could vote, Nixon resigned on 9 August 1974. Gerald Ford, his vice president, succeeded him and later pardoned Nixon of all crimes on 8 September 1974.

The resignation and pardon ended the political career of Richard Nixon, one of the country's most durable politicians. In the end, Richard Nixon became the only US president to resign because of character flaws that led him to cover up what he described as a "third-rate burglary."

Both Presidents Johnson and Nixon had some admirable qualities and achievements. However, both men were insecure and stubborn. Carrying out what he thought were his predecessor's policies, Johnson escalated a low-level conflict in Vietnam into a major war with tragic consequences including more than 58,000 US fatalities. Nixon reduced US force levels but utilized bombings that killed tens of thousands of innocent civilians to achieve leverage in negotiations. Nixon was forced to resign due to Watergate before the North Vietnamese took over the entire country in 1975.

I grew to despise Johnson's war policies, which I regarded as a betrayal of his 1964 campaign promises. I also grew to despise both Nixon's war policies, which expanded the war into Laos and Cambodia, and his personality. Both men led me to a cynicism about politics that, amplified by the Trump Administration, has continued to this day half a century later.

CHAPTER 8

January 1969: Computer technology

In 1971–1972, while an undergrad student, I did medical research in the Department of Human Genetics at the University of Michigan with Professor Donald Rucknagel. I studied whether a foetal form of haemoglobin, the oxygen-carrying pigment in blood, was associated with human cancers. I needed computers to statistically analyse the large amount of data.

During The Magical Decade, computer technology was still in its infancy. There were no personal computers, laptops or internet. Computers consisted of large mainframe machines that took up an entire room. Data was entered using stacks of thin cardboard punch cards (FIG 8-1). Results were printed on folding sheets of paper. There were no 'graphic user interfaces.' Computer programs were complex and rare.

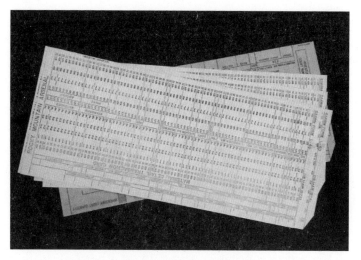

FIG 8-1: Computer punch cards from the collection of David Chudwin.
(Photo credit - David Chudwin)

I remember entering my research data into stacks of punch cards, which I carried very carefully in a box to the computing centre at the medical school (dropping the box and spilling the cards would have been disastrous because all the data would have had to be re-entered). The computer occupied a full room. I dropped off the cards and the next day picked up the printed results. The computer was connected to others on campus but not elsewhere.

This was because in the mid-1960s, computers could not communicate with each other over long distances. One of the main advances during The Magical Decade was the development of early versions of the internet whereby computers around the world could 'talk' to each other.

More than any other individual, information visionary Robert 'Bob' Taylor was responsible for the internet by developing ARPANET, its predecessor, for the US Department of Defense. In 1965, Taylor moved from NASA to the military's Advanced Research Projects Agency (ARPA), where he eventually became head of the Information Processing Techniques Office (IPTO). At that time, Taylor's office had separate computer terminals connected to ARPA-sponsored computers at MIT, UC Berkeley and SDC in Santa Monica. Each terminal had a community of users but there was no interconnectivity.

Taylor, a pioneer in electronic communications, realized the importance of the ability of these computers and their users to communicate with each other. In February 1966, Taylor persuaded ARPA director Charles Herzfeld to fund a computer network to link these computers together. The project was called ARPANET. Taylor was named director of IPTO in June 1966 and led ARPANET until 1969.

This February 1966 decision at the beginning of The Magical Decade for ARPA to develop a computer network was one of a series of advances in computer technology.[45] For example, another key development in 1966 was the first Hewlett-Packard commercial computer using integrated circuits (the HP 2116A).

The space program provided an impetus for computer miniaturization. The Apollo Guidance Computer (AGC) was developed to make it possible for the US to reach the Moon in the 1960s (See Chapter 9). In contrast to mainframe computers, which occupied an entire room, AGC was just 24 x 12.5 x 6.5 inches and weighed 70 pounds (FIG 8-2).

FIG 8-2: Apollo Guidance Computer DSKY keyboard.
(Photo credit - NASA)

AGC was developed by the MIT Instrumentation Laboratory.[46] The first AGC flew in space in 1966 aboard an uncrewed Apollo mission. Eventually, there was an AGC in the Apollo Command Module that orbited the Moon and another one in the Lunar Module that landed on the Moon's surface.

Astronauts entered command nouns and verbs into the AGC utilizing a display and keyboard interface (DSKY). The computer used a 16-bit word length. The memory was only a 2048-word RAM magnetic-core memory, and a 36,864-word ROM core rope memory. There is far more memory in the personal electronics of today, including smartphones or smartwatches, than in the AGC.

The Magical Decade also produced major advances in personal electronic equipment. Three groundbreaking examples included the first hand-held calculators, electronic quartz watches and, in 1975, the first primitive personal computers.

Both in high school and college I used a slide rule for advanced calculations. Slide rule belts were a telltale sign of scientists and engineers. Years later, when I found my old slide rule in the garage, my then-teenage son and daughter had no idea what the device was for or how to use it (FIG 8-3).

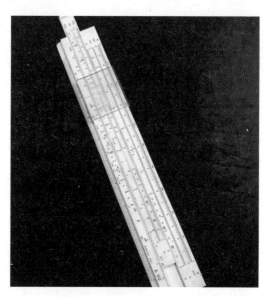

FIG 8-3: Slide rule from the collection of David Chudwin.
(Photo credit - David Chudwin)

In 1972, Hewlett-Packard went on to develop the first shirt-pocket sized calculator, the HP-35.[47] The 3.2 x 5.8-inch electronic calculator was able to do trigonometric and exponential functions, unlike the larger desktop calculators of that time, which could only do addition, subtraction, multiplication and division. The HP-35 became a bestseller among engineers and scientists, with over 100,000 sold in the first year at a list price of $395 (about $2,875 in 2023 dollars).[47] Soon these hand-held HP calculators went on to replace slide rules to the point that slide rules disappeared, except in museums (or my garage).

At about the same time, the first commercial personal electronic quartz watch was released in December 1969 by the Japanese company Seiko. Known as the Seiko Quartz-Astron 35SQ, the watch used a quartz oscillator, an integrated circuit and a tiny motor to turn the hands. It had a small battery with a lifespan of about one year. Seiko claimed the watch was accurate to one minute in a year. Previous traditional watches, used for centuries, were powered by springs that had to be hand wound daily.

The last year of The Magical Decade, 1975, marked the release of the first personal computers, sold initially as kits for hobby projects. The MITS Altair 8800 appeared at the start of the year.[48] A *Popular Electronics* magazine article detailed the computer and allowed people to order kits. Over 10,000 kits were sold for the primitive computer, which had a memory of only 256 bytes. The kit cost $439 (about $2,730 in 2023 dollars). A fully assembled model sold for $621 ($3,600 in 2023 dollars).

The same year (1975), Bill Gates and Paul Allen founded a company they named Microsoft to market a computer operating system called BASIC, which they modified for the Altair 8800. Their company became the leader in computer operating systems, and they became billionaires.

These events of The Magical Decade ignited the Computer Revolution, which has changed our world, including computer miniaturization, memory expansion, development of sophisticated operating systems, inclusion in devices ranging from telephones to automobiles, and the beginnings of Artificial Intelligence.

When I completed doing medical research 20 years later in the 1990s, there were no longer any punch cards, no mainframe computers were needed for most medical research, and I could communicate and share information over the internet with colleagues around the world. You may even be reading this on an electronic device right now. Personal computers, the internet and resulting social media have each become integral parts of Baby Boomers' lives since their origins during The Magical Decade.

CHAPTER 9

July 1969: Winning the Space Race

On the morning of 16 July 1969, I got up at 4:30 am to drive from the Sea Missile Motel in Cocoa Beach, Florida to the NASA Apollo 11 Press Center in Cape Canaveral. It was humid, dark, and the only sounds we heard were the chirping of crickets.

My friend Marvin Rubenstein and I had NASA press credentials to cover the Moon launch for the college press. I had just turned 19 years old five days before. We were the first college journalists to be fully accredited by NASA as such for a launch (a few other teenagers worked for professional media outlets).

We boarded buses in the dark with about 200 other reporters. The buses took us through the gates of the Kennedy Space Center to a roped-off area across from the Manned Spacecraft Operations Building (MSOB), where the astronaut quarters and suiting areas were located. (The MSOB is now called the Armstrong Operations and Checkout Building.) We ran from the bus to get the best possible vantage point.

Dawn arose and at about 6:25 am we could see activity through the open door of the MSOB. Soon the astronauts in their white space suits came to the front entrance, Neil Armstrong leading the way, followed by Michael Collins and Buzz Aldrin.

They waved and Armstrong gave a thumbs-up as they walked down the ramp to their 'astro van' for the trip to Pad 39A, where their Saturn V rocket awaited. There were cheers, applause and flashes from cameras as the astronauts and their retinue of space suit technicians, firemen and NASA officials approached the van. Elbows were flying as other photographers and I jostled to get clear shots of the men.

It was all over in a few minutes, but it was one of the high points of my trip to see Armstrong, Collins and Aldrin take their last steps on Earth before leaving to land on the Moon. How I ended up covering the first Moon landing mission at age 19 is a long story, recounted in more detail in my book *I Was a Teenage Space Reporter: From Apollo 11 to our Future in Space* (LID Publishing, 2019).[49]

The year 1965, at the start of The Magical Decade, marked a turning point in the Space Race between the United States and Soviet Union. Up until that point, the Russians achieved one space first after another. The Russians shocked the world when they launched the first artificial satellite, Sputnik, into Earth's orbit on 4 October 1957. The Russians had a penchant for secrecy, never announcing failures and never foreshadowing their future moves. The 'beep beep beep' radio sound transmitted by Sputnik was a wake-up call to the West. The US accelerated its space efforts and launched its first satellite, Explorer 1, on 31 January 1958.

The launch of Sputnik and Explorer 1 awakened in me an interest in space exploration that has persisted my entire life. I have traced that interest to several factors. First, my father had been an astronomy buff since his teenage years. He ground a glass mirror for a telescope while he was in high school and was a dedicated photographer with his own amateur darkroom. He instilled in me a curiosity about science and astronomy. Second, I was a voracious reader, even at a young age, of science fiction novels by writers such as Robert Heinlein and Isaac Asimov (see Chapter 20). Finally, nonfiction books such as Willy Ley's *Space Pilots* (1958) and television series (1955–1957) such as *Disneyland* produced by Walt Disney, in collaboration with former German rocket engineer Wernher von Braun, portrayed realistic plans for space travel in the near future.

There was a political uproar that the Soviets with Sputnik had beat the US in an important scientific and engineering endeavour during this competitive period of the Cold War. Along with other children, I did 'duck and cover' drills during school, although it was never clear to me how crawling under a desk would help protect me from a nuclear bomb. The US responded to the Russian space achievements by establishing the National Aeronautics and Space Administration (NASA), which opened for business in October 1958.

The first US spacemen, the Mercury 7 astronauts, were introduced to the public in April 1959 with the immediate goal of sending one of them into space, first on a parabolic suborbital flight and later to orbit the Earth. They were all male, military test pilots, as ordered by President Dwight D. Eisenhower. Like many youngsters then, I idolized America's first astronauts.

Again, the Soviets struck first with the launch of Major Yuri Gagarin as the first human in space on 12 April 1961, with a one-orbit flight around the world. I was 11 years old and deeply disappointed that an American was not first in space.

The US lagged behind as the Soviets reached one space milestone after another – the first simultaneous two crewed spacecraft missions (Vostok 3 and 4 in 1962), the first woman in space (Valentina Tereshkova in 1963), and the first human spacewalk (Alexei Leonov in March 1965), among others. (Years later I met Tereshkova and Leonov in person when they were in the US for two autograph shows). Importantly, the Russians had more reliable and more powerful rockets. I remember television newscasts in the early 1960s of spectacular explosions of US rockets destroying valuable unmanned payloads.

The year 1965, at the beginning of The Magical Decade, marked a turning point for NASA and the US space program. The initial crewed flight in March 1965 of the two-man Gemini capsule (Gemini 3) was the first time a spacecraft was able to change its orbital plane, a manoeuvre essential for rendezvous in space. Gus Grissom and John Young successfully put Gemini 3, informally known as 'Molly Brown,' through its paces. The next Gemini flight in June, Gemini 4, featured the first American spacewalk by Edward White.

The Gemini 4 crew visited Chicago afterwards.[50] My friend Marv and I were able to get tickets from our school to attend a special program for high school students.

The astronauts walked near us as they answered questions from the floor of the McCormick Place theatre. Jim McDivitt and Ed White were the first, but certainly not the last, astronauts I would meet in person. It was exciting to see and hear from them just a few weeks after their flight. I remember thinking how pale they both looked, probably from long hours in dark flight simulators. They received an enthusiastic welcome in Chicago with a parade and reception. They were accompanied by Vice President Hubert Humphrey and other NASA officials.

The next flight, Gemini 5, occurred at the same time in August 1965 that my family moved from Chicago to the suburbs. It was a long-duration (at least for that era) mission with the informal motto "Eight Days or Bust!" It was successful despite fuel cell problems that threatened to end the mission early.

Throughout this time, the Russians had beaten the US in one space first after another – first satellite, first animals in space, first human in space, first woman in space, first multiple crewed spacecraft in orbit and first spacewalk, among others. The tide began to turn with Gemini 3's ability to change its orbital plane but especially with the Gemini 6 and 7 missions.

Gemini 6 was supposed to attempt the first space rendezvous and docking with an uncrewed Agena target rocket (rendezvous is for two space vehicles to come in close proximity, and dock is to physically attach). However, the original mission was cancelled when the uncrewed Atlas-Agena rocket exploded after launch in October 1965. With another Agena target unavailable for months, mission planners came up with the ingenious idea of combining Gemini 6 and the planned long-duration Gemini 7 flight, using Gemini 7 as the target.

Gemini 7, with Frank Borman and Jim Lovell aboard, was launched first on 4 December 1965. Eleven days later, Wally Schirra and Tom Stafford lifted off from the same launch pad in the Gemini 6 spacecraft. Through a series of rocket firings, Schirra and Stafford changed their orbit to intersect with that of Gemini 7. The two Gemini spacecraft manoeuvred to within two feet of each other, achieving the first close-up rendezvous of crewed space vehicles. They got so close that pictures from the other spacecraft showed faces of crewmen and gag signs such as 'Beat Army' from the naval crew members.

The mission was a great success, augmented by spectacular colour pictures of the two Gemini spacecraft. The combined Gemini 7/6 mission was followed by the first planned docking flight with astronauts Neil Armstrong and Dave Scott. An hour and 41 minutes after their target Atlas-Agena was sent into orbit, the Gemini 8 crew blasted into low Earth orbit on 16 March 1966. The crew caught up with the Agena target vehicle and then docked for the first time in history. They attached the nose of their Gemini 8 capsule to the Agena a little more than 7 hours after launch.

About 27 minutes later, the combined Gemini-Agena spacecraft began to rotate rapidly. This uncontrolled roll reached a dangerous rate of one revolution per second. Dave Scott told me years later that he and Neil started to feel dizzy, had blurred vision and were on the verge of passing out. Doing some quick troubleshooting, Armstrong undocked from the Agena and fired the re-entry control system (RCS) rockets to stop the rotation. Later investigation showed that one of the Gemini spacecraft attitude rocket thrusters had been stuck open (roll thruster number 8).

Once the RCS rockets had been fired, the mission rules required the astronauts to return to Earth. Instead of the planned landing in the Atlantic, they had to make an unscheduled landing in the Pacific. I remember watching this unfold on television and was struck by the uncertainty of where they would end up in the vast Pacific Ocean. However, Armstrong and Scott were safely picked up by the USS Mason about three hours later.

The Gemini 8 mission proved that two spacecraft could rendezvous and dock in space – a function required for any future missions to the Moon. It also burnished the reputation of Neil Armstrong for his flying abilities and cool head as he methodically and calmly took action to save himself, Dave Scott and the mission.

My next chance to meet astronauts in person came with the next flight, Gemini 9. Tom Stafford was the commander, and the pilot was Eugene Cernan. Gene was from Bellwood, Illinois, a suburb of Chicago. The flight was to be another attempt at an Agena docking and also an ambitious spacewalk – or EVA – by Cernan.

Through no fault of the astronauts, the mission did not go smoothly. The Agena target blew up after liftoff and the mission was postponed until a new docking target could be constructed. When the new target was launched on 3 June 1966, a payload shroud was incompletely jettisoned. As the astronauts approached a few hours later, Tom Stafford exclaimed it looked like "an angry alligator."[51] No docking was possible, although they did achieve a close rendezvous.

Gene Cernan's spacewalk was also problematic. Without the hand and foot restraints later found to be essential, he had difficulty accomplishing his tasks. His heart rate and temperature went up and he began sweating profusely. He had to end what he called "the space walk from hell" early because of medical concerns he would pass out.[51]

Despite these difficulties, Stafford and Cernan received hero's welcomes on their return to Earth. A parade and public talk were scheduled in Cernan's hometown of Bellwood, a suburb of Chicago. I wrote to the mayor for tickets for Marv and me, but he replied none were necessary.

Marv and I had a chance to talk to the astronauts just before the parade and Tom Stafford autographed a copy of the parade route for me. They looked older than their years, with Stafford almost bald and Cernan with greying hair. We later attended a question-and-answer session for the public with them and Cernan's family at Proviso East High School. A report of their visit in the *Chicago Sun-Times* the next day included a picture of the crowd, with Marv and me clearly visible.[52]

Fast forward to December 1968. The Gemini program had concluded in 1966 with three additional flights that perfected spacewalking techniques and rendezvous and docking manoeuvres. In January 1967, the space program suffered a tragic loss as astronauts Gus Grissom, Ed White (whom I had met in 1965) and Roger Chaffee perished in a fire during a ground test in their Apollo capsule. The fire was due to flammable materials in a 100% oxygen atmosphere in the capsule. Many engineering and testing changes were made in the Apollo spacecraft to allow a successful crewed Apollo 7 mission in Earth orbit, commanded by Walter Schirra, in October 1968.

The next flight, Apollo 8, was scheduled to be an Earth orbital test of the Lunar Module (LM), the spider-like spacecraft that was to land astronauts on the Moon. It was also to be the first manned flight of the mammoth Saturn V Moon rocket. However, LM production and testing at Grumman on Long Island, New York, was running way behind schedule.

George Low, the brilliant, Austrian-born Apollo spacecraft program manager, came up with the idea of using the Saturn V to send the Apollo 8 Command and Service Module (CSM) to orbit the Moon without a LM. Astronauts Frank Borman, James Lovell and William Anders became the first humans to leave low Earth orbit (LEO) and enter deep space, as they were launched on 21 December 1968 and reached the Moon three days later.

Besides the engineering accomplishments, Apollo 8 had a great impact on the public psyche. Bill Anders took an iconic colour picture of 'Earthrise,' as our cloud-speckled, blue planet peeked above the bleak lunar surface. This picture has been called the most influential image of the Apollo program, showing Earth as small, fragile and without political boundaries. The picture became a symbol of the environmental movement (see Chapter 11).

The other major event was the scheduled Christmas Eve television broadcast from lunar orbit. No one knew what the astronauts were going to show or say, and there was anticipation around the world as hundreds of millions of people watched. The astronauts beamed fuzzy pictures of the Moon as they described the lunar surface. Then, as they approached the terminator, where they would go from light to darkness, Bill Anders began to read, "In the beginning, God created the heavens and the Earth ..."[53] Each astronaut read a few of the first verses of Genesis, describing the biblical creation. Mission commander Frank Borman then closed with, "And from the crew of Apollo 8, we close with goodnight, good luck, a Merry Christmas – and God bless all of you, all of you on the Good Earth."

I remember I had tears in my eyes as the broadcast ended. The scenes of the stark lunar surface coupled with the creation story from Genesis was perfect for the Christmas season. The broadcast was a huge success and was a fitting positive end to what otherwise had been a terrible year in 1968, with the assassinations of Martin Luther King, Jr. and Robert Kennedy, the death of Yuri Gagarin in an aeroplane accident, race riots, and cultural revolutions in China and Western countries. Frank Borman received a congratulatory telegram: "Thank you, Apollo 8. You saved 1968."[54]

While I was home in Illinois over the Christmas holiday, I was able to have some long conversations with Marv Rubenstein. He suggested, now that we were 18, we undertake a trip to Cape Kennedy over the summer to see a Saturn V launch. Upcoming missions included Apollo 9 in March to test the LM in LEO and Apollo 10 in May, which would be a full dress rehearsal for the Moon landing. If all went well, which was not for certain, the Apollo 11 flight scheduled for July would be the first attempt at a Moon landing.

July would be right in the middle of our summer breaks from college, so we aimed for Apollo 11. I decided to hold off making travel arrangements until the Apollo 9 and 10 flights were accomplished. However, I suggested to Marv that we should try to get press credentials for the mission, knowing that they would provide unequalled access to the launch.

The first hurdle was to get the approval of *The Michigan Daily* senior editors to represent the newspaper. *The Daily* had a long tradition of sending reporters to major out-of-state events (usually political ones), but I was just finishing my freshman year and was low on the totem pole. The other barrier was that *The Daily* had a limited travel budget and sending a reporter to cover a rocket launch was not high on the list of priorities.

In my favour was the fact that no one more senior than me had much interest in space, and I offered to finance the trip myself without any added funds from *The Daily*. With that proviso, I was given permission to represent *The Daily* at the scheduled Apollo 11 launch.

A much harder barrier to overcome was to persuade NASA to grant press credentials to Marv and me. The space agency regarded college journalists as students and generally did not accredit them. I thought I had hit a brick wall. As my hopes dimmed, I found out that Jim Heck, one of *The Daily* senior editors, was going to Washington, DC to be the summer editor of the College Press Service, a consortium of over 500 college newspapers. Jim agreed to plead my case in person to NASA Public Affairs, arguing that I would be covering

Apollo 11 for the entire college press and not just a single college newspaper.

Jim must have been persuasive, because I got a letter from him, dated 17 June 1969, that Marv and I would be receiving NASA press credentials to cover Apollo 11 for the College Press Service Wire Network. I checked the mailbox each day and was overjoyed when the press badges arrived.

After the success of Apollo 9 and Apollo 10, all was set for Apollo 11 to attempt humankind's first landing on the Moon. Astronauts Neil Armstrong, Michael Collins and Buzz Aldrin were scheduled to launch on 16 July 1969.

After the Apollo 10 crew splashed down on 26 May, I called the Sea Missile Motel in Cocoa Beach, Florida and made room reservations for $10 a night ($83 in 2023 dollars); I received a postcard confirmation postmarked 31 May (this was how reservations were made in the pre-internet era). I then made airline reservations on 2 June to fly from Chicago to the Melbourne, Florida Airport on 13 July, three days before the scheduled launch.

The trip began auspiciously as Marv and I arrived at the Eastern Airlines ticket counter at O'Hare Airport. We found we were coincidentally travelling on the same plane as Mrs Rose Cernan, mother of astronaut Gene Cernan, who was also going to see the Apollo 11 launch. Marv and I recognized her from the Gemini 9 event we had attended three years earlier, and briefly talked with her and her daughter Dee at the ticket counter.

The flight to Florida was uneventful, and after a stop in Tampa, we arrived at the Melbourne Airport.

Mrs Cernan was greeted by astronaut Alan Bean, who was picking her up because her son was busy, and three other men. Mrs Cernan asked what colleges we attended and then introduced us to Bean, who in turn introduced us to astronauts Jim Irwin (in a blue NASA flight suit), Charles Duke and Bruce McCandless.

So within 20 minutes of landing in Florida, we met three of the 12 men who would later walk on the Moon (Bean, Irwin and Duke), and the first untethered space-walker (McCandless).

The next three days were a blur of tours of the launchpad, vehicle assembly building (VAB), and launch control centre, where we were allowed on the floor of two of the three firing rooms. We got within 2,000 feet of the 363-foot-tall Saturn V (FIG 9-1), as well as being able to tour inside and on top of the roof of the VAB. We attended press conferences with the heads of NASA centres, including space pioneers Wernher von Braun, Robert Gilruth, Kurt Debus and George Mueller, the head of manned spaceflight with whom we later had a 20-minute private interview. We saw the rollback of the gantry structure around the Saturn V and then the 'bird' illuminated at night by high-intensity xenon lights (FIG 9-2).

FIG 9-1: Apollo 11 Saturn V on Pad 39A on 14 July 1969, two days before launch. (Photo credit - David Chudwin)

FIG 9-2: The author at dusk in front of the Apollo 11 Saturn V on 14 July 1969. (Photo credit - David Chudwin)

After witnessing the crew 'walk out' in their space suits on 16 July, we headed on NASA buses to cover the launch (FIG 9-3). There were big traffic jams that morning, so it took a while to get to the Launch Complex 39 Press Site, where hundreds of photographers and journalists were setting up. We saw another NASA bus leaving for the VIP Site and jumped aboard.

FIG 9-3: Neil Armstrong, Michael Collins and Buzz Aldrin walk out on 16 July 1969 from the crew quarters on their way to the first Moon landing. (Photo credit - David Chudwin)

NASA had invited over 5,000 guests to the launch, a 'who's who' of American society ranging from former President Johnson to TV personalities Johnny Carson and Ed McMahon. They assembled in three low grandstands at the VIP Site, which was the other side of the VAB from the Press Site.

Marv and I watched the launch itself from a grassy area in front of the VIP grandstands. We were a little over three miles from the Apollo 11 Saturn V – the closest the public was allowed without risking injury or even death if the Saturn V exploded.

The countdown went smoothly and at precisely 9:32 am EDT, a bright dot appeared at the base of the Saturn V. Flames and smoke shot out to either side of the launch pad, deflected by a series of trenches and concrete wedges. The rocket just seemed to sit there silently for a few seconds until liftoff. Then the sound waves began to hit us, pounding at our chests with a thunderous roar (FIG 9-4).

FIG 9-4: Launch of the Apollo 11 Saturn V as viewed by the author from the VIP Site about three miles away.
(Photo credit - David Chudwin)

It seemed to take minutes for the Saturn V to very slowly elevate above the pad; in actuality, it took ten seconds to clear the launch tower. As the rocket rose into the partially cloudy blue sky, we could actually feel the heat from the five F-1 engines producing 7.5 million pounds of thrust. The sound was overwhelming – a crackling roar. It pounded our chests and shook the ground under our feet.

After a couple of minutes, the Saturn V carrying Armstrong, Collins and Aldrin was just a dot of light in the sky heading for the Moon. To say experiencing in person the Apollo 11 launch from three miles away was exciting or thrilling or exhilarating would be an understatement. It was a life-changing experience for me.

While Marv flew back to Chicago, I decided to stay at the Cape for the landing, which I witnessed on 20 July 1969, at the NASA Apollo 11 News Center. Loudspeakers brought the assembled journalists air-to-ground communications and mission commentary from NASA.

The last eight minutes of the descent were perilous as computer alarms, boulders in the planned landing field and dwindling fuel challenged Neil Armstrong. With his usual calm and his experienced piloting skills, he landed LM Eagle successfully. "Houston, Tranquility Base here. The Eagle has landed," Armstrong radioed. Capsule Communicator (CAPCOM) Charlie Duke replied, "Roger, Tranquility, we copy you on the ground. You've got a bunch of guys about to turn blue. We're breathing again."[55] Years later, General Duke would write an advance praise for my book *I Was a Teenage Space Reporter*.

I had tears of joy in my eyes after the successful landing, thinking of President Kennedy, who set the goal to land on the Moon, the Apollo 1 crew, who gave their lives in the fire on the launch pad, and more than 400,000 American workers, tradesmen, scientists and engineers who had worked so hard to achieve the goal.[56]

After their successful mission, the Apollo 11 crew visited Chicago on 13 August 1969 and, using my NASA press credentials, I covered their triumphant ticker-tape parade, viewed by an estimated million people.[57]

There were many other space achievements during The Magical Decade. After Apollo 11, there were five additional Apollo Moon missions between 1969 and 1972. All safely landed and returned from the Moon, except for Apollo 13. On the way to the Moon, an oxygen tank exploded in the Service Module, cancelling the landing and forcing use of the LM as a 'lifeboat' to get the crew back to Earth. While Apollo 13 astronauts Jim Lovell and Fred Haise did not land on the Moon, many consider Apollo 13 NASA's finest hour, as the astronauts, flight directors, contractor employees and others on the ground united with quick ingenuity, determination and perseverance to bring the men back safely.

After the Apollo Moon flights were completed with Apollo 17 in December 1972, there were three crewed flights aboard Saturn 1B rockets to the Skylab space station in Earth orbit in 1973–1974. These were the first truly long-duration US space missions, with astronauts Jerry Carr, Ed Gibson and Bill Pogue spending 84 days in space aboard Skylab during the final flight.

The last space mission during The Magical Decade was the Apollo-Soyuz Test Project (ASTP) in July 1975. Astronauts Tom Stafford, Deke Slayton and Vance Brand docked their Apollo spacecraft in Earth orbit with a Soyuz capsule piloted by cosmonauts Alexei Leonov and Valery Kubasov. This was the first joint US-Russian space flight. The successful mission paved the way for future international cooperation with the space shuttle, the Russian Mir space lab and eventually the International Space Station.

The years 1965–1975 brought many important milestones in space exploration. These included the first active rendezvous (Gemini 7/6), the first space docking (Gemini 8), the first spacewalks (by Alexei Leonov and Ed White), the first astronauts to leave Earth (Apollo 8), and the first crewed landing on the Moon (Apollo 11).

I had an intense interest in space, triggered by Sputnik and ignited by being an eyewitness to Apollo 11. In the half-century since then, the space program has changed greatly, but it was those years in The Magical Decade in which the US achieved dominance in space.

The US and its partners have built upon the successes in space achieved during The Magical Decade. The International Space Station has now been continuously occupied for more than 23 years, the multinational crews performing important research.

The Artemis program to return to the Moon plans to bring men and women there in a sustainable way. The crew of the first Artemis landing mission will include the first woman and first person of colour to walk on the Moon. Led by the US, there are also plans for a Gateway space station in lunar orbit and for a lunar base. While it won't happen soon, a lunar colony is possible as the costs of launching to the Moon drop with developing rocket technology, such as Space X's Starship. The first major milestone in the Artemis program was the uncrewed flight of an Orion spacecraft around the Moon and its successful return to Earth in November 2022.

When the Apollo 8 crew was once asked if the Moon was made of cheese, Bill Anders replied, "Yes, American cheese!" However, future endeavours in space, besides Americans, will also include contributions by Canada, Japan, European countries and others. For example, India and the United Arab Emirates are developing countries with vigorous space programs. Baby Boomers of whatever nationality can be proud of their past and future accomplishments in space.

CHAPTER 10

November 1969: Protests in the streets

My first experience covering national protests against the Vietnam War was during the November 1969 Moratorium March on Washington (FIG 10-1).[58] I joined a half dozen *Daily* reporters to cover the protests, driving down from Ann Arbor, Michigan, in the backseat of a car. We stayed overnight in a tent in the backyard of one of our *Daily* contingent who lived in a Washington suburb.

FIG 10-1: Buttons promoting the November 1969 March on Washington from the collection of David Chudwin. (Photo credit - David Chudwin)

There was a dramatic 'March Against Death' beginning on Thursday night 13 November 1969. Marchers carrying candles and signs with the names of individual war casualties walked single file from Arlington National Cemetery to the White House and then on to the Capitol building. The marchers walked silently, grouped state by state, until near the White House. Once there, each protester called out the name of the dead person they represented. Their signs were then deposited in symbolic coffins at the Capitol. The solemn procession continued into the next day.

I covered the State of Michigan delegation for *The Daily*. There were an estimated 12,000 Michigan marchers, many of them young but also university professors, labour leaders and politicians. My report on the Michigan role in the 'March Against Death' appeared in the 14 November 1969 issue of *The Daily*.

My brush with the law was Friday, the following night. I was in the neighbourhood around DuPont Circle, close to the Vietnamese Embassy. The South Vietnamese regime manned the Embassy, and the site was often a target of anti-war protests.

I went out to an early dinner with friends at one of the many Asian restaurants in the area. Afterwards I caught up with a band of demonstrators heading toward the Embassy. Slogans were chanted and later some projectiles were thrown at police by a few of the militants, although the vast majority of the protesters were peaceful. I stayed clear of the troublemakers as I walked on the periphery of the demonstration. Outnumbered police attempted to keep the protesters away from the Embassy. Without warning, tear gas grenades went off.

This whitish gas hung in the air and then wafted away on the wind currents.

Even though I was at the edge of the crowd and started to run away, I got a powerful whiff of the tear gas. My eyes burned and watered like they never had before. I started coughing hard and my lungs hurt. A feeling of nausea gripped me as I tried to avoid throwing up. Running away from the fumes, I sought to find a water fountain to rinse my eyes. Later I learned that cow milk would have been more effective. The worst of the symptoms were over in a half hour. From the experience, I understood why 'professional' protesters carried gas masks. Tear gas and pepper spray were painful and were to be avoided if at all possible.

My second, and potentially more perilous, experience reporting anti-war protests occurred on 3 May 1971. Anger against the Vietnam War had intensified across America. I was again in Washington, DC for *The Michigan Daily* to cover the planned May Day anti-war protests designed to shut down the capital city.[59] In the early afternoon I was at a rally site near the imposing Department of Justice (DOJ) building adjacent to the National Mall.

Phalanxes of police in riot gear surrounded the DOJ complex. Protesters gathered and started chanting anti-war slogans. The police officers first advanced slowly, shoving back the mainly young anti-war activists with their batons. Then an order was given, and police accelerated their advance. Groups of policemen surrounded individual demonstrators, pushing them to the ground with fists and batons if there was any sign of resistance.

They subdued the protesters and then handcuffed them with ties around their wrists. By the hundreds, they were hauled away. The police indiscriminately arrested anyone on the streets in the vicinity of the DOJ. I had a *Daily* press pass but knew that it would be ignored – the police were doing mass arrests first and then asking questions later.

I looked around and saw the Smithsonian Museum of Natural History about a block away. With the police headed in my direction, I quickly ran down 10th Street to the Constitution Ave. entrance of the museum and managed to enter. I decided to transform myself into a 'tourist' and began to study the *Tyrannosaurus Rex* skeleton near the back entrance to the museum on 10th Street.

I had short hair, was clean shaven and wore a buttoned-down shirt, unlike most of the long-haired, bearded, T-shirt-clad protesters. I was staring up at the skeleton when a few police burst into the entrance and started looking around for demonstrators. My heart was pounding as I intently studied the dinosaur skeleton.

My 'disguise' must have been pretty good because some police officers ran by me as I tried to ignore their presence. They quickly left after apprehending several demonstrators. It took a few minutes for my heart to stop pounding.

More than 12,000 people were indiscriminately arrested that day, including my fellow *Daily* reporters Paul Travis and Lindsay Chaney.[59] They were herded into enclosures hastily established at the RFK football stadium and other venues. Lawyers for the ACLU and other groups went to court to get them released on *habeas corpus* grounds. A federal judge ordered the detainees to be released unless the police had evidence of specific crimes. It was a matter of luck, and the

Smithsonian Museum of Natural History, that I was not among them. Even today I have warm and fuzzy feelings when I see a *T. rex* skeleton!

Covering the March on Washington in 1969 and May Day in 1971 were two of the many anti-war activities I reported for *The Daily*. Years later I found that I had been a target of the Michigan State Police 'Red Squad' for 'crimes' such as attending an anti-war rally at Hill Auditorium in Ann Arbor where Jane Fonda was one of the speakers. A lawsuit led to the release of heavily redacted Michigan State Police files; I received mine months later, which revealed nothing criminal on my part but also that there had been police 'spies' undercover in the anti-war movement.

I was on a first-name basis with Ann Arbor Police detective Lt. Eugene Staudenmaier, who was assigned to keep track of campus 'radicals.' He tried to ingratiate himself with *Daily* staff and made it a point to hang out regularly in civilian clothes at the Student Publications Building at 420 Maynard Street. I engaged in small talk with Staudenmaier but did not trust him, well aware that he was a police detective.

As with almost all *Daily* staffers, I was against the Vietnam War. I had felt betrayed when Lyndon Johnson, who ran as the 'peace candidate' in 1964, ramped up US involvement in Vietnam with increasing American troops and casualties (see Chapter 7). I was against the war for numerous reasons. First, the US should never have gotten involved in what was basically a civil war between the North and South. Two dictatorial regimes were vying for power in the remnants of the French colonial empire. The US had never done well militarily in civil wars where deep-seated local animosities from past generations were more important than fragile recent alliances.

Second, the basic rationale for US involvement (to protect the US from communism) was faulty. There was never a communist monolith. The Russians, Chinese and Vietnamese all hated each other for historical reasons. The Sino-Soviet rift during this time was a prime example when the two powerful countries almost went to war in 1969. The Vietnamese were historically suspicious of the Chinese, whose Han emperors invaded Vietnam and ruled it for a millennium until the year 939. The 'domino' theory of communist aggression was questionable, especially after the downfall of Khrushchev in 1964.

Third, the US was waging the war with bizarre rules of engagement, tying the hands of commanders on the ground. Targets such as dams, railroads and harbours in the North were off-limits to US forces for fear of involving the Soviets or Chinese. There was a misguided emphasis on 'body counts' as a measure of progress. This led to an inevitable increase in civilian casualties, who were considered 'collateral damage.' Out-of-touch commanders at the Pentagon made battle decisions with insufficient input from US troops on the ground. All these mistakes led to an often-chaotic situation on the ground for the 'grunts' who were counting down their days left 'in country,' and praying they did not fall prey to Viet Cong ambushes or booby-traps.

Finally, there was an inherent unfairness in a military draft system where the wealthy got college deferments or phony medical rejections (such as Donald Trump's flat feet) while the poor were drafted and sent to 'Nam. A draft lottery was instituted in 1970, but inequalities remained with local draft board deferrals. (My lottery number was 263 out of 365. Because the highest number called in 1970 was 215, I did not have to make tough decisions about going into the military. My two brothers had even higher safer numbers.)

The Vietnam War sparked protests across America and around the world. The first 'teach-in' against the war was held by professors and students at my alma mater, the University of Michigan, in March 1965.[60] About 50 professors originally planned a one-day strike to protest the war, but then it was suggested to 'teach-in' instead of walking out. Overnight lectures, debates and forums marked the sit-in. The next month, representatives from colleges around the country met to plan teach-ins at their own campuses, igniting a wave of campus activism.

I was in high school during the initial wave of anti-war demonstrations in 1965–1967. Our teachers, with just a few exceptions, seemed to be supporters of President Johnson and the war. My gym teacher, a tough former football player from Texas, vowed he was going to get us into good physical condition so we would be fit to serve in Vietnam.

The first major national protests against the Vietnam War occurred in 1967. The National Mobilization Committee to End the War in Vietnam (known as the 'Mobe') was a coalition of anti-war groups. Their first mass protest was on 15 April 1967 in Central Park in New York City.[61] A huge crowd, estimated at 100,000 people, turned out to hear speakers such as Dr Martin Luther King, Jr., paediatrician Dr Benjamin Spock, and actor Harry Belafonte. The assemblage then marched to the United Nations Plaza. The protest was so successful that the organizers planned a more militant fall 1967 protest in Washington, DC, which became 'The March on the Pentagon.'

On 21 October 1967, a crowd estimated at 70,000 or more gathered near the Lincoln Memorial in West Potomac Park to listen to folk singer Phil Ochs, Dr Spock and activist David Dellinger.[61] More than half the crowd, led by hippie Abbie Hoffman, headed toward the Pentagon. They were met there by troops and US marshals. More than 650 demonstrators were arrested, including author Norman Mailer, who chronicled his experience in his Pulitzer Prize-winning book *The Armies of the Night*.

The next mass protests against the war were in conjunction with the Democratic National Convention in my hometown of Chicago in August 1968. I had been volunteering in Chicago and suburbs with the campaign of Senator Eugene McCarthy but had to leave for college the week before the convention started. Otherwise, I would have been in the middle of the protests in Grant Park with more than 10,000 anti-war protestors.

While most of them were peaceful, rocks and bottles were thrown by a few, and Chicago police violently responded with billy clubs and tear gas.[62] They made mass arrests, indiscriminately hauling in all those in the area. They burst into the McCarthy headquarters where I had been the week before and beat and arrested some of those present. These actions were later described by an investigative commission as a 'police riot.' The events surrounding the DNC further radicalized the mainly peaceful demonstrators.

The largest anti-war event in history occurred the following year in 1969.[63] As described above, I was tear-gassed the night before as I covered the events for *The Daily*. The 15 November 1969 Moratorium March on Washington brought over 500,000 people to the National Mall to hear singers Peter, Paul and Mary, Pete Seeger, John Denver and Arlo Guthrie perform music, and to hear speeches by Coretta Scott King, Senator Eugene McCarthy, Dr Spock and former Supreme Court Associate Justice Arthur Goldberg, among others.

One anti-war protest event that hit me particularly hard was the killing by Ohio National Guardsmen of four students at Kent State University in Ohio on 4 May 1970. The students were protesting the US invasion of Cambodia, which had been announced by President Nixon on 30 April.

I was driving down the expressway when I heard a news bulletin on the radio that Ohio National Guard troops had fired tear gas and live ammunition at a group of over 1,000 unarmed students at Kent State. Four young people were later reported dead, and nine others wounded, including one paralysed. I was shaking and almost in tears as I heard the news. I had to pull over to the side of the highway for a couple of minutes to regain my composure. I was angry at the use of deadly force by the Ohio Guardsmen and deeply shocked and saddened at the loss of life. I could have been one of those murdered students, I thought to myself.

The photo in *Life* magazine of teenager Mary Ann Vechio screaming as she knelt over the body of student Jeffrey Miller is forever etched in my memory. The powerful image was snapped by photographer John Filo and later won a Pulitzer Prize.[64]

An investigation showed that 28 Guardsmen had fired 61 shots in a 13-second barrage, killing Miller, Allison Krause, William Schroeder and Sandra Scheuer. Later, a Presidential Commission on Campus Unrest, headed by former Pennsylvania Governor William Scranton, concluded in its September 1970 report:

> "Even if the guardsmen faced danger, it was not a danger that called for lethal force. The 61 shots by 28 guardsmen certainly cannot be justified. Apparently, no order to fire was given, and there was inadequate fire control discipline on Blanket Hill. The Kent State tragedy must mark the last time that, as a matter of course, loaded rifles are issued to guardsmen confronting student demonstrators."[65]

The Kent State Massacre had a strong emotional effect around the country. Musician Neil Young was deeply moved as he saw the pictures of the event in *Life* magazine shown to him by bandmate David Crosby. In a short time, Young wrote the iconic protest song "Ohio."[66] They met Graham Nash and Stephen Stills in Los Angeles, recorded the song in a studio, and released it 1 June in almost record-breaking time. When I think about the Vietnam War and that period, the memorable lyrics and music of "Ohio" bring back those feelings of anger and sadness.

Meanwhile, at *The Daily* in Ann Arbor, I became interested in 1970 in the classified military research the University of Michigan was performing for the Defense Department (DOD). *The Daily* had first covered this war-related research in 1967, before I arrived, revealing that researchers at the University's Willow Run Laboratories were engaged in electronic remote sensing research applicable to battlefield targets, including a million-dollar counter-insurgency project in Thailand.

As one of the few on *The Daily* staff with a scientific bent, I became interested in what had transpired since the university set up a committee in 1968 to study classified military research proposals. I pored over unclassified university documents, wrote to the Defense Department, and interviewed university officials, including some of the researchers.

The result was a four-part special I wrote for *The Daily* on secret military research 27–30 October 1970.[67] The first article, titled "'U' research: Bringing the war home," summarized the University of Michigan's close relationship with the Defense Department. The University had 42 grants totalling $5.6 million in 1969–1970 for classified research (equivalent to about $44 million in 2023 dollars).

FIG 10-2: "'U' remote sensing: Sight for war eyes," article about military research by the author in *The Michigan Daily* on 28 October 1970. (Photo credit - David Chudwin)

Subsequent articles described the remote sensing technology that had made the University of Michigan "the leading free world authority in surveillance technology," according to the DOD[67] (FIG 10-2). Another article gave the history of Willow Run Labs, where much of the research was done; I described a visit I made there. A final article examined the moral dilemmas of performing secret research that prevented open publication of the results. While the fruits of the military research could be used for worthy purposes such as environmental monitoring, the research also helped to target and kill soldiers.

The series was widely praised, including by the head of the university's news service, as being comprehensive and fair. A welcome yet unexpected result was that I was privately contacted by one of the two graduate students on the Classified Research Committee (CRC) and he agreed to serve as a source, providing me with minutes and grant summaries (these were nonclassified materials but had not previously been made public).

I wrote another series of two articles on 9–10 March 1971 concerning the University of Michigan's contributions to the new 'electronic battlefield' being deployed in Southeast Asia.[68] At that point, the university had over $10 million (about $75 million in 2023 dollars) in DOD research, half of which was classified. Using information from CRC minutes and project summaries and from a letter from the DOD describing the university's contributions, I detailed projects involving infrared (heat) and acoustic (sound) sensors, as well as side-looking radar.

"These contributions have been invaluable in research leading to systems and equipment for battlefield surveillance and target acquisition," the DOD letter stated.[68]

Partly as a result of my articles, there was a faculty backlash against the remaining military research at a time when the Vietnam War was still raging. Over a period of months, the faculty Senate Assembly debated tightening up restrictions on classified research. The Regents of the University of Michigan eventually adopted policies prohibiting secret research, side-stepping whether it was military or not.

The most recent version from 1993 reads in part:

"The University will not enter into or renew any grant, contract, or agreement that would restrain its freedom to disclose the existence of the document, the identity of any sponsor of the proposed research, or the purpose and scope of the proposed research.

The University normally does not accept grants, contracts, or agreements for research that unreasonably restrict its faculty, staff, or students from publishing or otherwise disseminating the results of the research."[69]

Willow Run Laboratories was spun off by the University in 1972 as the Environmental Research Institute of Michigan so it could do military research without University restrictions. By 1997, much of its assets were transferred to a for-profit enterprise, ERIM International, which was later bought by General Dynamics Corp. The remnants have been transformed by acquisitions into a health consulting firm.

While peace talks in Paris between the US and North Vietnamese dragged on, the battlefield situation in Vietnam worsened as President Nixon drew down US troop levels (see Chapter 7). The US announced that it would pull out the last of its forces from Saigon. On 29 April 1975, there were chaotic scenes as Americans, Vietnamese and other foreigners tried to escape the communist forces that had entered Saigon. A fleet of helicopters evacuated the last US troops and Vietnamese to US ships offshore.

US involvement formally ended on Wednesday, 30 April 1975. On that day, I was on Central Campus in Ann Arbor. As I was walking near the iconic Burton Tower, the carillon bells there started playing the old Civil War era folk tune "When Johnny Comes Marching Home" with a dirge-like, slow cadence. Transfixed, I sat down on one of the outdoor benches and listened, singing softly the familiar words:

When Johnny comes marching home again
Hurrah! Hurrah!
We'll give him a hearty welcome then
Hurrah! Hurrah!
The men will cheer and the boys will shout
The ladies they will all turn out
And we'll all feel gay
When Johnny comes marching home.

The old church bell will peal with joy
Hurrah! Hurrah!
To welcome home our darling boy,
Hurrah! Hurrah!
The village lads and lassies say
With roses they will strew the way,
And we'll all feel gay
When Johnny comes marching home.

Get ready for the Jubilee
Hurrah! Hurrah!
We'll give the hero three times three,
Hurrah! Hurrah!
The laurel wreath is ready now

To place upon his loyal brow
And we'll all feel gay
When Johnny comes marching home.

As this Civil War tune played with the bells slowly chiming, I became emotional as I thought of the 58,000 Americans, 1.1 million Vietnamese soldiers and up to two million civilians who had lost their lives and would not be coming home. I thought of the families who had lost their sons in the war, just as my grandparents lost my uncle killed in action during World War II. I thought of the billions of dollars that had been wasted in equipment, weapons, aircraft and bombs. I thought of the divisions in America the war had engendered, too often pitting the old against the young. What a useless, misguided war!

As the last few sad notes from the carillon reverberated on the campus, a tear fell down my cheek on the day the Vietnam War came to an end.

CHAPTER 11

March 1970: Saving the environment

On Wednesday, 11 March 1970, I was in Crisler Arena at the University of Michigan. The venue was packed with over 13,000 spectators. This was not a Wolverine basketball game nor a rock music concert. It was a new phenomenon – one of the first events that ushered in the environmental consciousness movement. I was there covering it in person for *The Michigan Daily*.[70] Because of my interest in science, I became the lead reporter on environmental issues.

It was the kickoff rally for the ENACT (Environmental Action for Survival) teach-in, a five-day event in March that led to the first Earth Day a month later on 22 April (FIG 11-1). There was an electric atmosphere in Crisler Arena as attendees understood this was an historical event, the formal start of a movement to Save the Earth. I could sense the enthusiastic and hopeful attitude of the crowd. They were mainly students but the audience also included faculty, politicians and community activists.

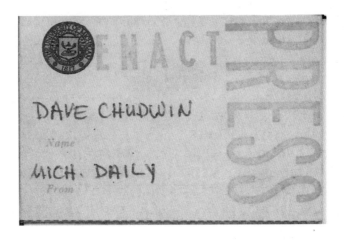

FIG 11-1: Press badge used by the author during the ENACT environmental teach-in in 1970, from the collection of David Chudwin. (Photo credit - David Chudwin)

I scribbled notes furiously as a series of speakers addressed the crowd. The keynote speaker was Senator Gaylord Nelson of Wisconsin, a pioneer in addressing environmental issues. He called for financial, social and ethical changes to meet the environmental crisis. Nelson was later one of the founders of Earth Day celebrations.

Others who spoke that night included ecologist Barry Commoner, entertainer Arthur Godfrey, Michigan Governor William Milliken and University President Robben Fleming.

In spring 1970, a student group that adopted the name ENACT had been formed to promote the nascent environmental movement. The group decided to hold a five-day teach-in at the University of Michigan to educate the public about environmental problems, causes and solutions.

The teach-in opened on 10 March with workshops and guerilla theatre in Ann Arbor. The next day, before the kick-off rally, there was a mock 'trial' of an automobile on the Diag, the central square of the University, on charges of pollution. After a guilty verdict, the car was sentenced to 'death' and was smashed by sledgehammers. I remember the sound of glass cracking as the windows of the sacrificial auto were bashed in.

On 13 March, there was a four-hour marathon panel about the causes of pollution, which filled Pioneer High School's auditorium and gym with a noisy audience of over 2,500 people. I also covered that event for *The Daily*. Senator Edmund Muskie of Maine was the principal speaker. Wearing a button reading "Give Earth a Chance," the Maine Democrat and future presidential candidate cautioned against using the environmental crisis as a 'smokescreen' for other issues. He warned against "the poisons of hate and fear that divide us and set us against each other."[70]

Muskie received a positive response, although he faced some radical hecklers in the audience. The brunt of the heckling, however, was for Walter Reuther, president of the United Auto Workers, and especially for Ted Doan, president of Dow Chemical Corp. Dow was widely reviled as a source of pollution in Michigan and elsewhere. Before the program there were guerilla theatre presentations outside Pioneer High School attacking Dow and Doan.

During the final day of the ENACT teach-in, consumer advocate Ralph Nader spoke to a capacity crowd of 3,500 in historic Hill Auditorium. He warned against 'corporate violence' and said corporations need to be accountable for pollution. That night a final summary panel discussion was led by Gary Mayor Gordon Hatcher, an African-American.

In a 2 September 1970 summary of this precursor event to Earth Day, I wrote in *The Daily*, "During those five days, this campus received one of the most massive doses of environmental education ever to be unleashed in this country."[70]

I was honoured to have had the opportunity to help cover this national event for *The Daily*. Before that time, I was not up to speed about environmental issues. However, the space program, in which I had a long-time interest, contributed to my understanding of the urgency of the environmental situation.

In particular, the view of Earth from the Moon affected the perspective not only of the 24 astronauts who voyaged to the Moon, but also those of us on Earth who saw the magnificent pictures they took.

The Apollo 8 crew, with their famous "Earthrise" photograph snapped by Bill Anders in December 1968, especially revolutionized public attitudes about the Earth. Seeing a small blue ball in the vast cosmos with a thin layer of atmosphere and no political boundaries gave a new environmental perspective (FIG 11-2). In fact, Stewart Brand's 1969 *Whole Earth Catalogue* featured the "Earthrise" photo on its cover.

FIG 11-2: "Earthrise" photograph taken by Bill Anders aboard Apollo 8 in December 1968.
(Photo credit - NASA)

Astronaut Jim Lovell talked about being able to cover up his view of the Earth by just holding out his thumb at a distance while twice flying around the Moon (Apollo 8 and 13). Astronomer Neil DeGrasse Tyson made the comment that, "We went to the Moon but discovered Earth."

Complementing crewed missions, unmanned satellites continue to provide vital data about the weather, storms, global warming, atmospheric changes, oceanography, earth resources, land use and crop conditions.

Observations by crews aboard the International Space Station (ISS) over the last two decades have provided dramatic examples of hurricanes, flooding, drought, air pollution and loss of glaciers. Astronauts aboard the ISS circle the Earth every 90 minutes at an altitude of about 250 miles at a speed of 17,100 miles per hour.

ISS and earlier astronauts were changed by the experience of orbiting the Earth. Frank White has popularized the term 'the overview effect' for this change in perspective. This overview effect is powerful. Astronaut Nicole Stott argues in her book *Back to Earth: What Life in Space Taught Me About Our Home Planet – And our Mission to Protect It* that we are all crew members and not just passengers on Planet Earth, and that only a thin blue line of atmosphere separates us from the deadly vacuum of space. She states our environment is fragile and requires maintenance and care (FIG 11-3).

FIG 11-3: Picture of the 'thin blue line' showing how thin the atmosphere surrounding Earth is. The photo was taken aboard the International Space Station. (Photo credit - NASA)

Down here on Earth, I had encountered a variety of environmental problems during The Magical Decade. Air pollution was one of the most visible issues I experienced. Some of the major sources of air pollution then and now are automobiles, factories and the energy sector.

My first car, a hand-me-down from my parents, was a 1974 Buick. It had horrible fuel efficiency – only eight miles per gallon (compared to up to four times greater efficiency today). Auto engines, such as those powering my Buick, were a major source of air pollution and smog, which was especially apparent in Los Angeles and other urban locations.

In 1970, the Environmental Protection Agency (EPA) was established by President Nixon and Congress. The same year, Congress passed the Clean Air Act, which called for a 90% decrease in auto emissions by 1975, including carbon monoxide, nitrogen oxide and hydrocarbons. The following year, 1971, the EPA began testing the fuel economy of cars and trucks.

In 1975, at the end of The Magical Decade, Congress voted to set fuel economy goals for new cars with the Corporate Average Fuel Economy (CAFÉ) program. Also in 1975, the first catalytic converters were built to reduce vehicle exhaust emissions. Finally, unleaded gasoline was introduced for 1975 models because the health hazards of lead began to be appreciated.

Besides automobiles, factories were another source of air pollution. When I lived on the South Side of Chicago, we were only a dozen miles west of the US Steel plant in Gary, Indiana. We would pass that grimy industrial complex driving east to the Indiana Dunes or Michigan. There was a foul odour in the air and chimneys belched smelly, toxic fumes. The Gary Works was a major cause of air pollution before environmental regulations.

Factory effluent also played a role in water pollution. A prime example was the Cuyahoga River in Ohio. I was in Cleveland in 1971 for a summer internship on the copy desk of *The Cleveland Press*. The river was foul smelling and the river had actually caught on fire due to industrial wastes in June 1969. This was not the first time the river had blazed, but the June 1969 fire made the Cuyahoga the poster child for river pollution in the U.S.

The energy sector contributed to pollution by burning coal, fuel oil and natural gas. During that time, electrical generating plants were largely fuelled by coal. One of the reasons nuclear power was developed was to reduce the use of dirty coal to produce electricity. Of course, nuclear power has its own environmental consequences. While modern coal-burning plants are more efficient, they still are important sources of air pollution. Fortunately, use of coal as a source for electricity has dropped by half in the last quarter century.

Home heating had transitioned in the 1950s and 1960s from coal to oil and then to natural gas. When I was a young child, there was an oil tank in the basement of our house in Chicago, which was filled each heating season. Our new house in the suburbs used natural gas – which burns more cleanly and is less polluting.

The Magical Decade marked a profound change in Baby Boomers' thinking about the environment as exemplified by the view of Earth from space. Air and water pollution, waste treatment, car and truck efficiency, and stewardship of the Earth became subjects of education and debate. Events such as the ENACT teach-in I covered in 1970 in Ann Arbor as a college journalist were the forerunners of a new environmental consciousness.

Regulations and laws passed during The Magical Decade have yielded tangible changes. These have included less air pollution, reduced reliance on coal for electricity, greater use of natural gas for heating, more efficient autos and trucks, cleaner lakes and rivers, and preservation of wetlands and their inhabitants. Whether some of these environmental protections should be rolled back was hotly debated during the Trump Administration. Topics such as the Keystone

Pipeline and offshore oil and gas drilling leases were again in the headlines, more than 50 years after The Magical Decade.

CHAPTER 12

March 1972: Equality for women

22 March 1972 was a momentous day for the American women's rights movement. On that day in The Magical Decade, the US Senate finally passed the Equal Rights Amendment (ERA) after years of debate. Such an amendment to the US Constitution was first proposed in 1921, but it was not approved by the House of Representatives until 1971 and the US Senate the following year. The text of the ERA was as follows:

"Section 1. Equality of rights under the law shall not be denied or abridged by the United States or by any State on account of sex.

Section 2. The Congress shall have the power to enforce, by appropriate legislation, the provisions of this article.

Section 3. This amendment shall take effect two years after the date of ratification".[71]

The US Constitution provided that constitutional amendments like the ERA would need to be ratified by legislatures of three-fourths of the states (38 of 50 states); a seven-year deadline for ratification was established in the enabling legislation. In the end, the ERA was only ratified by 35 states, falling three states short. It failed to be adopted after politically conservative groups mounted a successful last-ditch campaign against it.

The failure to ratify the ERA was emblematic of the difficult struggle American women faced for equal rights. The feminist movement in the US began in 1848 with a meeting in Seneca Falls, New York, organized by Elizabeth Cady Stanton and Lucretia Mott. The focus of this first wave of feminism was women's suffrage.

Women, more specifically White women (due to further additional discrimination against women of colour), did not have the right to vote in the US until August 1920, when the 19th Amendment to the Constitution became law. For centuries, while single women had legal rights to own property, married women were under the control of their husbands, who had title to their property. The right to vote was a hard-won victory for the women of that era (my paternal and maternal grandmothers were unable to vote until they were respectively 33 and 25 years old).

There was a second wave of feminism in the 1960s and 1970s. Betty Friedan's 1963 influential book, *The Feminine Mystique*, argued that women had identities beyond just childbearing and homemaking. A women's liberation movement developed to revolt against societal restrictions, most importantly those limiting advancement of women in the workplace.

When I grew up in the 1950s, women were expected to get married, have babies and stay at home to raise them, as well as caring for their husbands. Women who needed or wanted to work were generally limited to becoming nurses, teachers or secretaries. In each of these roles, they were subservient to male physicians, principals and executives, respectively. Women themselves in the professions – law, medicine, finance and the ministry, for example – were rare.

My own family was part of this patriarchal structure. Both of my grandfathers ruled the roost, with my grandmothers following their direction as homemakers. Neither of my grandmothers had their own careers (FIG 12-1). My mother met my father at the University of Wisconsin-Madison in 1945, where she was an undergrad and he was a medical student in military uniform. She sacrificed her college career to marry him in 1946 after she turned 20, and to accompany him to Philadelphia, where he served his medical internship.

FIG 12-1: The author's paternal grandmother with him as an infant in 1951. Like many women of that era, she did not have her own career. (Photo credit - David Chudwin)

She did not return to college until 1967 when, under the influence of the feminist movement, she resumed her studies and earned an undergraduate degree in 1971. She later garnered a master's degree in communications. She and a coauthor later wrote a book, *College After 30: A Handbook for Adult Students*, that was published in 1981 about their experiences returning to school.

After his civilian internship, my dad was stationed as a physician in the US Army Medical Corps in post-war

Germany from 1947–1949. While there, my mom worked as a secretary at the American military hospital in Frankfurt, one of the few jobs available to women. I was born in 1950 in Chicago after their return home and my mother chose to become a homemaker. This fit in with the traditional paradigm of the 1950s, where the father went to work while the wife stayed home to variously raise the children, decorate the house, hold dinner parties and cater to her husband.

My mother had three children in six years and moved from an apartment to two houses sequentially in Chicago within five years. Baby and household duties kept her very busy, especially since she did not have her own car the first years of her marriage.

The iconic television shows of the 1950s showed women as homemakers subservient to their husbands. Examples of these classic shows included *I Love Lucy* with Lucille Ball and Desi Arnaz; *The Honeymooners* with Jackie Gleason and Audrey Meadows; and *Leave it to Beaver* with Barbara Billingsley, Hugh Beaumont and their 'son' Jerry Mathers.

The 'glass ceiling' for women was exemplified by the selection of the first US astronauts in 1959. President Dwight D. Eisenhower ordered that the astronauts must be military test pilots. However, the US military did not allow women to become pilots of any type until 1977.

Dr Randolph Lovelace, who medically evaluated male astronaut candidates for NASA, wondered if women could pass the same physiological testing as men. Lovelace tested experienced female civilian pilot Jerrie Cobb in 1960 and she passed the difficult physical exams with flying colours. With private financial support,

Lovelace and Cobb decided to ask for female volunteers to undergo the same testing as the male 'Original 7' Project Mercury astronauts announced in April 1959. They sought women with at least 1,000 hours flying time as civilian pilots.

Lovelace and Cobb went through the flying and medical records of the women volunteers and, after extensive testing, came up with 13 women pilots who passed NASA astronaut medical qualifications. They became informally known as the 'Mercury 13,' even though they never became astronauts. (One of them, Wally Funk, at age 82 flew a suborbital mission on the first crewed New Shepard flight in July 2021). It was not until 1978 that NASA would name the first six women astronauts and not until 1983 that Sally Ride became the first American female astronaut in orbit.

Besides being barred from the astronaut corps, during the beginning of The Magical Decade there were very few women scientists, engineers, lawyers, business executives and politicians, among many other occupations. In response to this bias, the US Equal Employment Opportunity Commission (EEOC) was established by Congress in 1964. The Commission began its work in 1965 to help enforce Title VII of the 1964 Civil Rights Act, which forbade discrimination based on gender.

However, progress was slow because ingrained sexist attitudes were hard to change. As mentioned above, I grew up in a traditional, male-dominated family with two brothers and no sisters. Looking back, as I went through grammar school and high school, I held sexist views, although I was not cognizant of this bias at the time. There were several very smart girls in my classes, but I still thought of them as second-class citizens. My role models were male sports figures, actors and astronauts. I did not see many women to look up to (other than my mother and other female family members).

I did not realize how sexist I was until I joined the staff of *The Michigan Daily* in Ann Arbor during my freshman year in college. I worked closely there with several brilliant women on the editorial staff. On at least a couple of occasions, however, I was called out about my male chauvinism. My behaviour was unconscious in the sense that I did not even realize the situations when I was making sexist statements, discounting the opinions of females on the staff, or treating females subordinately. I listened seriously to these complaints about me and tried to change my behaviour. I would note that I was not the only male on *The Daily* staff with male chauvinist, sexist tendencies.

When it came to the advancement of women on *The Daily*, we did appoint a woman, Sara Fitzgerald, as my successor as managing editor, and she later became the first peace-time female editor-in-chief. She went on to a distinguished journalism career with *The Washington Post*.

By the time I entered the University of Michigan Medical School in 1972, times had started to change and nearly half our medical student class was female. There was still sexism and discrimination, however, in some departments, especially the surgical specialties. There were few female surgical residents and they faced harassment from their male colleagues and superiors.

However, there were also female medical pioneers in Ann Arbor at the time. For example, Alexa Canaday, who had worked as feature editor of *The Daily*, became the first female African-American neurosurgeon in history, as noted in Chapter 2. Professor Elizabeth Crosby, a distinguished neuroanatomist, became the first female full professor at the University of Michigan Medical School in 1936 and was still active in the 1970s when I was in medical school. She walked around with a crutch but continued to do anatomy research into her 80s. In 1980, Professor Crosby received the National Medal of Science in person from President Jimmy Carter at the White House. She died in 1983 at the age of 94.

As The Magical Decade progressed, significant milestones were made in ending discrimination against women. Attitudes change slowly, however, and it was not until 1978, as noted above, that the first female American astronauts were selected; not until 1981 that Sandra Day O'Connor was nominated as the first female associate justice of the US Supreme Court; and not until 2020 that Senator Kamala Harris was elected the first female Vice President of the US.

One medical advance that greatly changed the status of women was the development in the 1950s and 1960s of contraceptives for women. Under the leadership of Margaret Sanger and her organization, the American Birth Control League (later renamed Planned Parenthood), researchers sought to develop an oral birth control pill containing progestins and estrogens. The first pill (Enovid) was approved to control menstruation in 1957, but many women used it for its contraceptive 'side effect.' Finally, in June 1960, the FDA approved Enovid for female contraception.

By 1965, the start of The Magical Decade, 6.5 million American women were using oral contraceptives.[72]

However, religious and conservative groups opposed the use of 'the pill' as immoral. In this context, as discussed in Chapter 4, the US Supreme Court in 1965 ruled in *Griswold v. Connecticut* that married women had a right to use oral contraceptives;[24] this was extended to unmarried women in *Eisenstadt v. Baird* in 1972. In these and related cases, the justices created a right to marital privacy that forbade the government from interfering with personal decisions such as the use of contraception.

The pill and other forms of contraception such as intrauterine devices gave women more control over their own bodies by allowing them to separate sex from pregnancy. Women could decide to have sex without the fear of getting pregnant, liberating their sexuality. The mantra of 'free love' espoused by the hippies was made possible, in part, by the development of easily obtainable female contraception.

The availability of contraception also had a profound effect on female employment. The ability of female employees to time pregnancies reduced the 'risk' to employers of unplanned pregnancies. While not entirely attributable to the pill, the number of women in the workplace tripled between 1965 and 2015.

During The Magical Decade, use of female contraception skyrocketed. This ability of women to determine their own pregnancies, along with their increased political rights, led to a sea change in the status of women around the world.

However, it will likely take decades for male chauvinism to recede and for women to be truly accepted as equals. During The Magic Decade, my own attitudes about women's equality also changed, especially during my years at *The Michigan Daily* in 1968–1972. While I may not have been a 'male chauvinist pig,' I do admit to sexism then in both attitudes, words and actions. I am grateful to my female colleagues there for pointing out my transgressions, and I trust I have progressed and learned from them.

CHAPTER 13

April 1972: Human rights

In 1972, well into The Magical Decade, the radical left Human Rights Party (HRP) in Ann Arbor, Michigan, ran two candidates for City Council. One was Nancy Wechsler and the other was my friend Jerry DeGrieck. While only briefly on the staff of *The Michigan Daily*, Jerry hung out at 420 Maynard St., *The Daily* headquarters, and dated one of the female staffers. We were the same age and both interested in politics, although he was more radical than me. At the time, I was finishing my undergraduate degree (BS in zoology) and starting medical school.

The HRP was founded in Ann Arbor in 1970 as a response to the traditional Democrats and Republicans. HRP was a socialist party, composed mainly of students, that aspired to represent workers as well. HRP was vehemently against the Vietnam War, opposed capitalism, and promoted the rights of women and other minorities.

One previously silent minority across the US was the homosexual community, which became more commonly known as the gay community. For decades, homosexuals suffered abuse because they were considered 'immoral' and 'unnatural,' due to the biblical verses against same-gender relations.

Gay male sex was illegal then in all US states. Sodomy (oral or anal sex) was a felony with harsh punishments. In 1962, a proposed model national penal code finally removed homosexual sex in private between consenting adults as a crime. My home state of Illinois was the first state to adopt that code in the same year.

Over the next four decades, anti-sodomy laws were repealed or overturned in 36 states. In the others enforcement was spotty, but in some jurisdictions these laws were used to threaten and discriminate against gays and bisexuals. In June 2003, the US Supreme Court in *Lawrence v. Texas* overturned Texas' sodomy law.[73] In a 6–3 decision, the Court ruled that sodomy laws involving private sexual conduct among adults violated the Due Process clause of the US Constitution.

Besides struggling for legal rights, the gay community began to assert itself publicly during The Magical Decade, with events starting with the 'Stonewall Riots' in June 1969. Gay patrons of the Stonewall Inn, a gay bar in Manhattan, revolted against police as the cops tried to raid the establishment and arrest its largely gay clientele. This was one of the first times gay men stood up and publicly resisted police harassment. Militant groups such as the Gay Liberation Front were organized afterwards, and Gay Pride events such as parades and festivals were held in June of subsequent years to commemorate the Stonewall uprising.

At the beginning of The Magical Decade in 1965, however, homosexuality was still considered a mental illness.

It was not until 1973 that the American Psychiatric Association removed homosexuality from its DSM book of psychiatric disorders.

In the political arena, when White House aide Walter Jenkins was arrested in 1964 after having sex with a man in a YMCA changing room, he checked into a hospital. Jenkins, who was married to a woman, was fired by President Johnson, but Johnson's wife Lady Bird issued a sympathetic statement: "My heart is aching today for someone who has reached the end point of exhaustion in dedicated service to his country ... He is now receiving the medical treatment he needs."[74] She framed Jenkins' situation as a medical problem and not an issue of sexual orientation.

In 1965, when I was in high school, there was disdain for and discrimination against homosexuals. I was aware of just one gay male student at my high school, who also was a neighbour. While he was not open about his homosexuality, he was bullied and called epithets such 'faggot' or 'queer.' Indeed, one of the worst insults used against male students at the time was 'faggot.'After high school, he came out and moved to San Francisco.

Back in Ann Arbor, in April 1972 the HRP nominated Nancy Wechsler and Jerry DeGrieck for City Council seats (FIG 13-1). Their electoral districts (Wards 1 and 2) were primarily student areas, and they won their elections. Their victories were unexpected because they represented a new and somewhat radical third party. Gay rights were not a prominent issue in their campaigns, although supporting gay liberation was certainly part of the platform of the HRP.

FIG 13-1: Election bumper sticker of Human Rights Party candidate Nancy Wechsler. She won election to the Ann Arbor City Council and later came out as gay, one of the first US public officials to do so. From the collection of David Chudwin. (Photo credit – David Chudwin)

However, the next year, anti-gay harassment in a local bar led to a news conference in which both DeGrieck and Wechsler publicly came out as gay. As such, they were the first elected public officials in the US to publicly acknowledge their homosexuality. They predated gay rights pioneers such as Harvey Milk, who was elected to the San Francisco Board of Supervisors in 1977, running as a gay man.

Neither DeGrieck nor Wechsler ran for reelection when their terms were up in 1974. Wechsler moved to Boston and continued as an activist. DeGrieck moved to Seattle, where he left the public arena and worked for the Seattle Department of Health. Back in Ann Arbor, openly gay Kathy Kozachenko ran for Wechsler's seat on the Council in 1974 and won, becoming the first openly LGBT politician to win an election in the United States.

One of the other barriers the gay community faced was their inability to marry the person they loved. Same-sex marriage was illegal in the 1960s, and civil unions between same-sex couples did not exist. The Netherlands in 2001 became the first nation to establish same-sex marriage, also called marriage equality.

In the US, the first state to recognize same-sex marriage was Massachusetts in 2003. A number of states followed; however, it was not until 2015 that the US Supreme Court ruled on the matter. In the landmark case of *Obergefell v. Hodges*, the Supreme Court decided 5–4 that the Equal Protection and Due Process clauses of the 14th Amendment permitted same-sex couples to marry with the same conditions as opposite-sex couples.[75] This ruling invalidated state bans on same-sex marriage and established marriage equality as the law of the land.

However, those who had fought for marriage equality during The Magical Decade could not celebrate their victory for long. Justice Clarence Thomas' comment in 2022 in the *Dobbs* abortion case, questioning the privacy basis of the *Obergefell* decision, raised concerns that a more conservative Supreme Court could also reverse marriage equality. To prevent this, Congress passed the Defense of Marriage Act the same year, requiring states to recognize legal marriages performed in any other state.

Another area where gay people faced discrimination before and during The Magical Decade was the US military. Previously, any serviceman or woman who was found to be gay was discharged from the military under Section 8 of Army penal code. Section 8 was used to separate men who were considered mentally unfit to serve. Despite this, gay people did enter the military and hid their sexual orientation. This abnormal situation created tensions that affected morale, not the least of which was the opportunity for blackmail.

In September 2011, the ban on openly gay men or women serving in the military was removed. President Barack Obama said in a statement, "As of today, patriotic Americans in uniform will no longer have to lie about who they are in order to serve the country they love. As of today, our armed forces will no longer lose the extraordinary skills and combat experience of so many gay and lesbian service members."

The latest frontier for gay equality has been discrimination against transsexuals. Transgender individuals are those whose gender identity does not match their assigned birth gender. For example, a trans woman was born a man and then transitioned with the help of surgery and hormone treatment to become a woman. Conversely, a trans man was born a woman and then transitioned with hormones and surgery to become a man.

In civilian life, there have been controversies in schools regarding participation of transgender students in interscholastic athletics, since trans women are perceived to have an advantage, having been born male. In general, males physiologically are stronger and have more muscle mass due to the effects of testosterone.

School districts, states and the Olympics have all taken different views, with some jurisdictions requiring sex testing, others setting levels of maximum blood testosterone, and others allowing students to compete based on their own self-identity.

In the military, acceptance of transgender troops was approved by President Obama in 2016. However, a later Pentagon policy ordered by the Trump Administration prevented them from enlisting or serving as of April 2019. This policy was overturned in the first days of the Biden presidency when he signed an executive order on 21 January 2021, again permitting transgender individuals to enlist and serve openly.

In 2023, several state legislatures controlled by Republicans passed laws banning 'gender affirming care' for transgender individuals under 18. The trans community had become a lightning rod in the culture wars waged by conservatives.

Despite this, acceptance of gay Americans as citizens has advanced greatly since the beginning of The Magical Decade. At that time, their sexual orientation was considered criminal, there was no same-sex marriage equality, and homosexuality was grounds for dismissal from the military. I was in Ann Arbor in 1972–1973 when the first two openly gay politicians, including Nancy Wechsler and Jerry DeGrieck, were members of the City Council. In the years since then, the arc of justice for gay individuals has continued to expand, although they still face discrimination in some conservative parts of the US.

CHAPTER 14

January 1973: Foetal viability and abortion

The baby came by ambulance in 1979 from Northern Wisconsin, but this was no normal newborn. He was only 28 weeks gestation, born three months early to a woman who happened to be a nurse. I was astounded at how small he was, weighing in at about 2.2 pounds and only 14 inches long. What was also remarkable was that this extremely premature infant was breathing on his own and not requiring a ventilator.

I was training in paediatrics at the University of Wisconsin School of Medicine, where I was doing a required rotation in the neonatal intensive care unit (NICU). It was located at Madison General Hospital and comprised several large rooms with incubators to provide warmth, oxygen, feeding, and protection against infection for premature babies. The rooms were somewhat noisy with the beeping of IV machines, ventilators and heart rate monitors.

Strides in neonatal medicine in the 1970s and 1980s allowed survival of premature newborns who never would have lived in earlier years. A better understanding of neonatal physiology, coupled with technological advances in ventilator technology, reduced the birth age of premature babies who could survive on their own from 30 weeks gestation in the 1960s to about 26 weeks when I was in the NICU in 1975. (Full-term pregnancies are 40 weeks.)

The gestational age at birth that a newborn has a chance of survival by himself or herself is called *foetal viability*. With further progress in neonatal medicine, that age has in recent years dropped to 23–24 weeks.

The notion of foetal viability has important clinical consequences with respect to perinatal resuscitation of very premature babies. If a newborn has no chance of survival, it is considered ethically wrong to subject the foetus to invasive procedures such as intubation, IVs and arterial lines. The common practice is to provide comfort and care and allow these tiny, nonviable infants to die naturally without subjecting them to invasive resuscitation.

During my NICU rotation, I was struck by this degree of change in the age of foetal viability. Most babies who would have never survived in the previous decade at 30 weeks gestation were doing well. Since my paediatric training in the 1970s, this line of foetal viability has continued to improve, although at a slower rate than during The Magical Decade. There has also been a decrease in long-term sequelae of extreme prematurity such as cerebral palsy, blindness and lung damage. Besides the clinical significance of foetal viability, it also has ethical and legal importance, especially in the abortion debate.

On 22 January 1973, the Supreme Court of the United States in *Roe v. Wade* issued a landmark decision about the legality of abortion.[25] In a 7–2 decision written by Justice Harry Blackmun, the Court stated that the right to privacy in the Fourteenth Amendment is: "broad enough to encompass a woman's decision whether or not to terminate her pregnancy" (see Chapter 4).

The Court decided that the trimester of pregnancy, and hence foetal viability, should control the degree to which the state could interfere with that right. With this 'trimester framework,' *Roe v. Wade* weighed the competing interests of the woman's privacy-derived right to decide to terminate her pregnancy versus society's interest in protecting both the health of the mother and the life of the foetus.

In the first trimester (gestational weeks one to 12), when there is zero chance of foetal viability, the Court held that the woman's choice was paramount and that the right to abortion could not be prohibited. The Court struck down in 1973 the Texas and Georgia laws that outlawed abortion except when the woman's health was threatened.

During the second trimester (weeks 13 to 28), the Court allowed regulation of abortion to preserve the health of the mother. However, it ruled that since the foetus was not yet viable (in 1973), the woman's right to terminate was still paramount.

During the third trimester (after 28 weeks) when foetuses might survive, the rights of the foetus were declared to be dominant, and the Court allowed abortion to be prohibited. The practical effect was to make abortion legal across the US during the first and second trimesters of pregnancy.

In a 1980 paper titled "The Limited Moral Significance of 'Foetal Viability,'" I and my coauthors Dr Norman Fost and Prof. Daniel Wikler argued that viability is not a solid basis for deciding the legality of abortion (FIG 14-1).[76] This is because the age of viability has changed through the years from 30 to 31 weeks gestation in the 1960s, to 24 weeks in 1973 when *Roe v. Wade* was decided, and to 22 to 23 weeks today. Medical advances have blurred the distinctions embodied in the trimester framework.

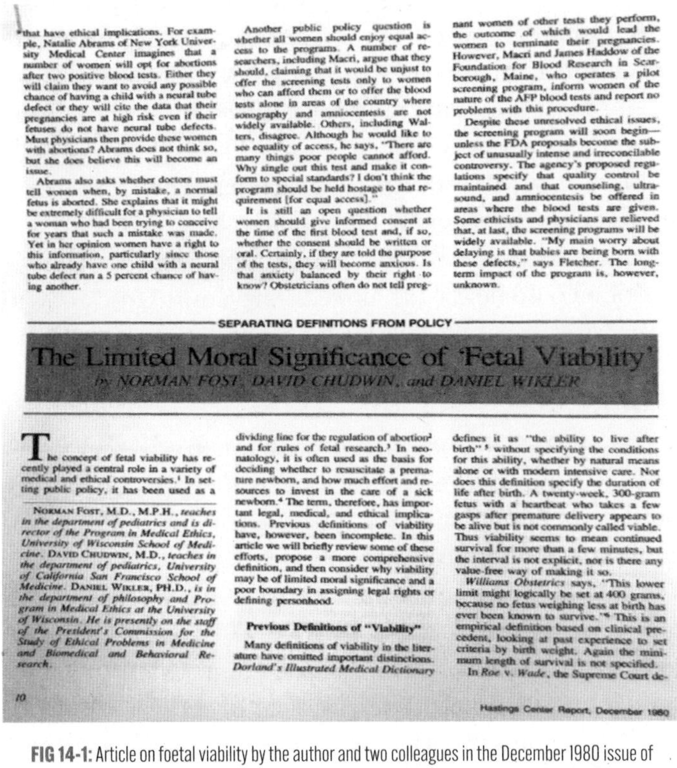

that have ethical implications. For example, Natalie Abrams of New York University Medical Center imagines that a number of women will opt for abortions after two positive blood tests. Either they will claim they want to avoid any possible chance of having a child with a neural tube defect or they will cite the data that their pregnancies are at high risk even if their fetuses do not have neural tube defects. Must physicians then provide these women with abortions? Abrams does not think so, but she does believe this will become an issue.

Abrams also asks whether doctors must tell women when, by mistake, a normal fetus is aborted. She explains that it might be extremely difficult for a physician to tell a woman who had been trying to conceive for years that such a mistake was made. Yet in her opinion women have a right to this information, particularly since those who already have one child with a neural tube defect run a 5 percent chance of having another.

Another public policy question is whether all women should enjoy equal access to the programs. A number of researchers, including Macri, argue that they should, claiming that it would be unjust to offer the screening tests only to women who can afford them or to offer the blood tests alone in areas of the country where sonography and amniocentesis are not widely available. Others, including Walters, disagree. Although he would like to see equality of access, he says, "There are many things poor people cannot afford. Why single out this test and make it conform to special standards? I don't think the program should be held hostage to that requirement [for equal access]."

It is still an open question whether women should give informed consent at the time of the first blood test and, if so, whether the consent should be written or oral. Certainly, if they are told the purpose of the tests, they will become anxious. Is that anxiety balanced by their right to know? Obstetricians often do not tell pregnant women of other tests they perform, the outcome of which would lead the women to terminate their pregnancies. However, Macri and James Haddow of the Foundation for Blood Research in Scarborough, Maine, who operates a pilot screening program, inform women of the nature of the AFP blood tests and report no problems with this procedure.

Despite these unresolved ethical issues, the screening program will soon begin—unless the FDA proposals become the subject of unusually intense and irreconcilable controversy. The agency's proposed regulations specify that quality control be maintained and that counseling, ultrasound, and amniocentesis be offered in areas where the blood tests are given. Some ethicists and physicians are relieved that, at last, the screening programs will be widely available. "My main worry about delaying is that babies are being born with these defects," says Fletcher. The long-term impact of the program is, however, unknown.

SEPARATING DEFINITIONS FROM POLICY

The Limited Moral Significance of 'Fetal Viability'

by NORMAN FOST, DAVID CHUDWIN, and DANIEL WIKLER

The concept of fetal viability has recently played a central role in a variety of medical and ethical controversies.[1] In setting public policy, it has been used as a dividing line for the regulation of abortion[2] and for rules of fetal research.[3] In neonatology, it is often used as the basis for deciding whether to resuscitate a premature newborn, and how much effort and resources to invest in the care of a sick newborn.[4] The term, therefore, has important legal, medical, and ethical implications. Previous definitions of viability have, however, been incomplete. In this article we will briefly review some of these efforts, propose a more comprehensive definition, and then consider why viability may be of limited moral significance and a poor boundary in assigning legal rights or defining personhood.

NORMAN FOST, M.D., M.P.H., *teaches in the department of pediatrics and is director of the Program in Medical Ethics, University of Wisconsin School of Medicine.* DAVID CHUDWIN, M.D., *teaches in the department of pediatrics, University of California San Francisco School of Medicine.* DANIEL WIKLER, PH.D., *is in the department of philosophy and Program in Medical Ethics at the University of Wisconsin. He is presently on the staff of the President's Commission for the Study of Ethical Problems in Medicine and Biomedical and Behavioral Research.*

Previous Definitions of "Viability"

Many definitions of viability in the literature have omitted important distinctions. *Dorland's Illustrated Medical Dictionary* defines it as "the ability to live after birth"[5] without specifying the conditions for this ability, whether by natural means alone or with modern intensive care. Nor does this definition specify the duration of life after birth. A twenty-week, 300-gram fetus with a heartbeat who takes a few gasps after premature delivery appears to be alive but is not commonly called viable. Thus viability seems to mean continued survival for more than a few minutes, but the interval is not explicit, nor is there any value-free way of making it so.

Williams Obstetrics says, "This lower limit might logically be set at 400 grams, because no fetus weighing less at birth has ever been known to survive."[6] This is an empirical definition based on clinical precedent, looking at past experience to set criteria by birth weight. Again the minimum length of survival is not specified.

In *Roe* v. *Wade*, the Supreme Court de-

10

Hastings Center Report, December 1980

FIG 14-1: Article on foetal viability by the author and two colleagues in the December 1980 issue of *Hastings Center Report* from the collection of David Chudwin. (Photo credit - David Chudwin)

Indeed, the Supreme Court, in the 1992 decision *Planned Parenthood v. Casey*, replaced the trimester framework with an 'undue burden' standard.[77] It ruled that restrictions on abortion could not place an undue burden on women seeking to terminate their pregnancies before the foetuses were viable. There was no explicit reliance on the trimester framework, but this new standard also emphasized the importance of viability, putting it centre stage in the debate.

Thus, the legality of abortion under *Roe v. Wade* hinged on the concept of viability. However, this formulation depends on the definition of viability. Viability, therefore, depends on the state of medical knowledge at the time. Furthermore, viability may differ in various other countries depending on their available medical technology. Thus, viability may be a poor boundary in assigning legal rights and personhood.[76]

Current medical practice is not to resuscitate newborns who are less than 22 weeks gestation or less than 400 grams birth weight, although there have been very rare instances of survival of extremely premature infants born below this boundary.

The whole debate about abortion is again in the headlines 50 years later with a new 6–3 conservative majority on the US Supreme Court. President Trump nominated three conservative Associate Justices (Neil Gorsuch, Brett Kavanaugh and Amy Coney Barrett) to the Court from January 2017 to January 2021. After heated hearings in the Judiciary Committee, the US Senate approved the controversial nominations before the end of Trump's term.

On 24 June 2022, the US Supreme Court, by a 6–3 vote, changed course on abortion, reversing *Roe v Wade* as wrongly decided, and returning abortion regulations to the states. The ruling, written by Associate Justice Samuel Alito, came in the case of *Dobbs v. Jackson Women's Health Organization*.[26]

As background about this decision, in 2018 Mississippi passed the Gestational Age Act, a law banning abortion after 15 weeks gestation, except where the health of the mother was at risk or for severe foetal anomalies. The only abortion provider left in the state, Jackson's Women's Health Organization, filed a suit stating the Mississippi law was unconstitutional. US District Court Judge Carlton Reeves ruled the law was, in his opinion, indeed unconstitutional and issued an injunction against its enforcement. The state appealed, but Reeves's ruling was upheld 3–0 by the Fifth Circuit Court of Appeals.

The US Supreme Court decided to take up a further appeal by the State of Mississippi of the Court of Appeals decision. The Supreme Court granted permission to review the findings of the lower courts in a writ of *Certiorari* issued in May 2021. In the writ, the court decided to limit the case to the question: "Whether all pre-viability prohibitions on elective abortions are unconstitutional."[26] Oral arguments in the case were heard on 1 December 2021.

In his 24 June 2022 decision in *Dobbs*, Justice Alito claimed there was no right to abortion in the US Constitution and he questioned the basis for other Court decisions based on privacy. This 6–3 ruling flew in the face of previous decisions, which is unusual for the Supreme Court, where the doctrine of *stare decisis* holds that settled law should not be reversed. The other major example in recent memory for such a reversal was *Brown v. Board of Education* declaring segregation illegal.

Decisions about abortion were returned to the states, where viability again plays a role in when to restrict abortions, whether at 15 weeks or earlier.

My experiences as a resident physician in the NICU in Madison kindled my interest in the concept of foetal viability due to the dramatic improvements in survival of extremely premature neonates during The Magical Decade. This trend has continued, albeit at a slower rate. Foetal viability became an important part of the impassioned abortion debate, which has continued in state legislatures as well as lower courts after the *Dobbs* decision by the Supreme Court.

CHAPTER 15

October 1973: Oil and the economy

It was 1973 and the line of cars stretched around the block, each driver eagerly waiting to get gasoline at a gas station in Ann Arbor. I sat in my car, waiting my turn at the pumps. What had once been a plentiful commodity – gasoline – was now scarce and more expensive, in part due to panic buying. While I remember that most people in the gas lines were patient, at times tempers flared.

The gasoline crisis of 1973–1974 and resulting inflation was the most important economic event of The Magical Decade. The saga started far away from the US, in the Middle East with the Yom Kippur War. The armies of Egypt and Syria invaded Israeli-occupied territory in Sinai and the Golan Heights, respectively, on 6 October 1973 in a surprise attack. The Israelis, aided by emergency supplies from the US, repulsed the invaders and gained some territory, but at a heavy loss of life. A new ceasefire was signed by the belligerents on 25 October 1973; however, the aftershocks of the war would last for years.

The Organization of Petroleum Exporting Countries (OPEC) had been founded in 1960 and was composed of largely Arab oil producers. The group was reluctant at first to use oil as a political weapon, mainly due to hesitancy by Saudi Arabia.

That situation changed with the Yom Kippur War. On 17 October 1973, in response to US and European aid to Israel during the war, the Arab members of OPEC agreed to use an oil embargo to protest Western support for Israel. The countries targeted at first included the US, UK, Canada, Netherlands and Japan. The embargo began on 20 October, the day after President Richard Nixon requested a $2.2 billion emergency aid plan for Israel from Congress.

Besides the embargo against specific nations, the Arab countries also announced a 25% cut in overall oil production on 5 November 1973. The result of the embargo and production cuts was that the price per barrel of oil in the US rose from its longstanding level of $3 per barrel to $12 per barrel, a fourfold increase. Gasoline at the pump in the US rose from 38 cents per gallon to 55 cents per gallon. Shortages of gasoline resulted in lines at the pumps in 1973–1974. American consumers at the time, including me, were upset both at the scarcity of gas and the increased price.

During 1974, there were ongoing negotiations between Egypt and the Israelis that led to Israeli withdrawals from Egyptian territory in November 1974. Afterwards, Arab foreign ministers, apart from Libya, ended the year-long embargo. However, by then there had been serious economic damage caused by the embargo. The dramatic increase in oil prices affected the US and worldwide economies. Prices for energy, manufactured goods, transportation and other sectors rose with resulting inflation.

The Magical Decade had started with a booming economy dating from 1962. The stock market rose steadily and reached an unprecedented Dow Jones Industrial Average level of 1,000 by January 1966. This prosperity was marked by increasing numbers of ordinary Americans investing in stocks, with a generation of Baby Boomers becoming rich.

There was also a trend in the 1960s of consolidations and mergers in many sectors of the economy. Corporate mergers and acquisitions took place as companies became large conglomerates. Small shops and family restaurants suffered as consumers switched to discount chain stores and fast-food restaurants. Family farms became less prevalent with the advent of large corporate farming. There was a shift in jobs away from manufacturing to service industries. Even with these changes, the years 1962–1968 marked a period of great prosperity for Baby Boomers, equalling the 'Roaring Twenties,' but without the Depression that followed. There were storm clouds on the horizon, however.

Problems with the economy had begun early in The Magical Decade with large US federal budget deficits due to spending for the Vietnam War and domestic Great Society programs. The US also had a negative balance of payments problem with foreign countries, creating a trade deficit. In addition, loose Federal Reserve monetary policies further promoted inflation.

The result was a drain on US gold reserves. For decades the US dollar had been valued at $35 per ounce of gold. The Bretton Woods agreement of 1944 had pegged exchange rates for international currencies such as the US dollar or pound sterling to gold with only narrow trading ranges.

The bullish stock market from 1962–1968 gave way to a moderate crash in 1969–1970 in the middle of The Magical Decade. The Dow Jones Industrial Average declined 36%, dropping from 906 in 1968 to 753 in 1970. At the same time, unemployment increased from 3.4% in 1968 to 6.1% at the end of 1969. Inflation and trade deficits ballooned further. The gold standard for the dollar became increasingly untenable, and in August 1971 President Nixon closed the gold window. He also instituted unprecedented temporary wage and price controls and a 10% import tax. These unexpected actions were known as the 'Nixon shock.'

A December 1971 attempt to repeg the dollar at $38 per ounce with a 2.25% trading band was a failure. By 1973, a new system of currency values was established as European countries and Japan decided to let their currencies float.

Partially because of these problems with the dollar, the US stock market went into a severe tailspin starting on 11 January 1973. During this serious stock market crash of 1973–74, the Dow Jones Industrial Average level dropped by 45%. Associated with the stock crash was a recession, with Gross Domestic Product (GDP) falling 2%. The recession was accompanied by significant inflation as the Consumer Price Index increased by 12%.

The oil crisis starting in October 1973 contributed to the recession, inflation and weak economy, but the stock market crash had begun in January long before any gasoline shortages. The 1973–1974 recession was one of the worst since the Great Depression in 1929.

I was in medical school then and definitely noticed the increase in prices due to inflation, with everything costing more. For example, the price of postage stamps increased from 5 cents in 1965 to 13 cents by 1975. Gasoline went from 30 cents per gallon in 1965 to 53 cents by 1975. When I went to the grocery store, prices for food and other items were noticeably higher. According to the US Bureau of Labor Statistics Inflation Calculator, goods and services that cost $100 in January 1970 had jumped to $146.83 in December 1975. At the end of The Magical Decade, the recession finally ended in March 1975, but unemployment remained stubbornly high at 9%.

The scourge of inflation would get worse in the late 1970s and early 1980s after The Magical Decade. The annual inflation rate reached nearly 15% in 1980 and was one of the reasons Ronald Reagan defeated incumbent President Jimmy Carter in the 1980 presidential election. 'Stagflation' was added to the economic vocabulary, with a combination of high inflation and unemployment coupled with stagnant demand.

What started off as a rosy economic picture during the mid-1960s ended up with an economic disaster as The Magical Decade was ending. The 1973–1974 oil embargo precipitated energy shortages and increased prices, which added to inflation. But even before the oil embargo, there were problems with the US economy. The lines at the gas pumps I witnessed in 1973 were the forerunners of a more serious decline in the

US economy in the 1980s, which negatively affected me and other Baby Boomers.

CHAPTER 16

April 1974: Sports

While there were many memorable sports events during The Magical Decade, perhaps the most historic was baseball player Henry Aaron breaking the all-time career home run record held by Babe Ruth. On 8 April 1974, playing in Atlanta, Hank Aaron surpassed the Babe's longstanding mark of 714 career home runs.

This was also a watershed moment in race relations in the US as Aaron, an African-American athlete, broke the beloved Babe Ruth's record. Aaron received jeers and vicious hate mail from racists, but also was the recipient of support and encouragement from teammates, the Atlanta Braves, and many baseball fans. I remember the vitriol directed at Aaron because of his race – a Black man had the 'temerity' to surpass one of America's greatest sports heroes.

Aaron had almost broken the record in 1973, and excitement mounted in anticipation of the next season. Finally, on 8 April 1974, at the Braves' Atlanta-Fulton County Stadium, he hit home run number 715 to eclipse the 'Bambino's' career home run tally.

Hank Aaron went on to play two more seasons for the Milwaukee Brewers, hitting his 755th and final home run on 20 July 1976. In later years, the widely revered Aaron returned to Atlanta, where he worked in the Braves' front office. He was elected to the Baseball Hall of Fame in his first year of eligibility and received the Presidential Medal of Freedom, the nation's highest civilian honour, in June 2002 from President George W. Bush, among many other awards. Aaron died at the age of 86 in 2021.

The Magical Decade in professional sports started off with a bang in May 1965 as boxer Muhammad Ali knocked out Sonny Liston in Lewiston, Maine, with a phantom punch in the first round of their fight. Ali ended Liston's hopes of regaining his world boxing championship after only one minute 44 seconds into the match. The swift victory cemented Ali's position as the top boxer in the world. In 1964, the year before, Ali had converted and joined the Nation of Islam, changing his name from Cassius Clay. He remained a controversial figure for becoming a Black Muslim and opposing the Vietnam War.

In other 1965 events, baseball great Willie Mays hit over 50 home runs, the second time he achieved that feat. The Los Angeles Dodgers won the 1965 World Series. In golf, Jack Nicklaus won the Masters golf tournament by nine strokes, while Gary Player became only the third golfer to win four major tournaments.

Sports news in 1966 was dominated by the world soccer (more commonly known as football internationally) championships. The FIFA World Cup was held in England with massive crowds in attendance. England, the host country, won the World Cup by defeating Germany in overtime in the final. I remember watching some of the matches on American television and the wild enthusiasm of the English fans. Also in 1966, a young female tennis star, Billie Jean King, won her first of many grand slam tennis championships at Wimbledon in England.

The year 1967 marked the first Super Bowl game for the US professional football championship. The Green Bay Packers defeated the Kansas City Chiefs on 15 January 1967, starting an annual sports tradition. I remember watching that first Super Bowl on television. I cheered for Kansas City because there was no love lost between Chicago Bears fans such as myself and the hated rival Green Bay Packers. I was disappointed the Packers won the first Super Bowl, a Packer victory that became an all-too-frequent event, at least from my perspective.

In 1968, the Summer Olympics took place in Mexico City in October. The United States won the most medals, including the most gold. Athletes, especially those used to living at sea level, had to deal with the high altitude of the venue (7,300 feet). The 1968 games will be remembered for the Black Power protest by two American athletes at the medal ceremony for the 200-metre sprint. Gold medal winner Tommie Smith and bronze medal winner John Carlos stood on the podium for the ceremonial raising of the US flag. As the Star-Spangled Banner was played, they lifted a black-gloved arm in a silent protest. I remember seeing pictures of this scene in all the newspapers and magazines.

This political statement by the two African-American athletes raised a furore. They were immediately criticized by Avery Brundage, long-time head of the International Olympic Committee, who stated that political gestures were not allowed during the ceremonies. Supporters of Smith and Carlos pointed out that the IOC under Brundage allowed German Olympians during the 1936 Olympics in Berlin to give the Nazi salute when receiving their medals. The IOC claimed that this was a national salute and not a political protest.

Brundage ordered Smith and Carlos suspended and removed from the Olympic Village. When the US Olympic Committee resisted, Brundage threatened to ban the entire track team. Bowing to pressure, the two African-American athletes were expelled from the games. Brundage and the IOC were accused of racism, while Smith and Carlos were criticized for politicizing the games.

The 1968 Winter Olympics were held uneventfully in Grenoble, France, with Norway winning the medal count. Back in the US, the Green Bay Packers won a second consecutive Super Bowl over the Oakland Raiders in a hard-fought game held in the Orange Bowl in Miami, Florida (as a Packer 'hater,' I did not approve).

In 1969, on 22 November, I was an eyewitness in Ann Arbor as the University of Michigan football team unexpectedly upset the number-one-ranked Ohio State Buckeyes. The Buckeyes had a 22-game winning streak and had widely been predicted to win. The Michigan Wolverines, under their new coach Bo Schembechler, prevailed 24–12 in front of a then-record 104,000 fans at a frigid Michigan Stadium. Both Michigan and Ohio State fans were stunned by the margin of the upset victory.

I was one of the delirious Michigan fans who stormed the field and tore down a goal post. I still have a piece of the goal post cover ripped from the uprights. I framed

my ticket stub to the historic contest as well (FIG 16-1).
The game, regarded as one of the best in college football
history, was the start of a fierce rivalry between Buckeye
coach Woody Hayes and Wolverine coach Schembechler.

FIG 16-1: Ticket stub from the collection of David Chudwin for the Michigan-Ohio State football game
in November 1969 when the Wolverines upset the Buckeyes. (Photo credit – David Chudwin)

Also in 1969, the New York Jets, led by flashy quar-
terback Joe Namath, upset the favoured Baltimore Colts
16–7 in Super Bowl III. I had previously seen the Jets play
in person in 1967 at an exhibition game in Connecticut
when I was attending a summer science program for
high school students.

The change of the decade in 1970 was marked by a
legendary NBA basketball championship finals series
between the New York Knicks and Los Angeles Lakers.
The Knicks won the series four to three games with

Game 7 considered one of the greatest Game 7 finals of all time. Injured Knick Willis Reed walked on to play part of the game, surprising the fans and his teammates by his participation, and gave the Knicks a boost as he guarded Wilt Chamberlain. Despite heroics by Jerry West of the Lakers, the Knicks were able to win 113–99 with 36 points from Clyde Drexler.

The big sports event of 1971 was the boxing match between heavyweight champions Joe Frazier and Muhammad Ali. It was known as 'The Fight' and was named one of the greatest boxing matches ever. Frazier defeated Ali in 15 rounds by unanimous decision on 8 March 1971, at Madison Square Garden in New York City. While Frazier won this first contest, Ali subsequently went on to defeat Frazier twice, in 1974 and 1975 (the 'Thrilla in Manila') (see below).

In 1972, the Summer Olympics in Munich, Germany was tragically marred by the deaths of 11 Israeli athletes and coaches, as well as a German police officer. They were held hostage by Black September Palestinian terrorists. The Israelis were killed after a botched rescue attempt by the Germans on 5 September at the Munich Airport. All but three of the Palestinian terrorists were also killed during the rescue; two of them were assassinated later by Israel's Mossad intelligence agency. The Olympic Games continued after a two-day pause and a memorial service for the slain Israelis. This tragic episode saddened me because once again Israelis were the target of terrorists.

In 1974, the Miami Dolphins defeated the Washington Redskins 14–7 in Super Bowl VII to complete the only perfect season in the history of the National Football

League (by the Dolphins) – no ties or losses. The event was held at Los Angeles Memorial Coliseum in California. Also in January, George Foreman knocked out Joe Frazier in the second round to win the heavyweight boxing championship. In golf, Johnny Miller won the US Open with a final round score of 63, a new record that lasted until 2017 for a total of 43 years.

Perhaps the greatest boxing match in history occurred in 1975, the final year of The Magic Decade. Muhammad Ali defeated Joe Frazier in the 'Thrilla in Manila' on 1 October to keep his heavyweight boxing championship. The bout took place in the Philippines and was the third and final match between the two great champions. Frazier had won their first meeting in 1965, but then Ali prevailed in the subsequent one. The fight in Manilla was a brutal one; Ali won by a technical knockout in the 14th round. An estimated billion people worldwide watched the match on television. Ali became a revered figure around the world. He later lit the torch at the 1996 Summer Olympics in Atlanta and was named Sportsman of the Century by *Sports Illustrated* and the BBC.

While I was not much of an athlete myself (right field was my permanent baseball assignment), I was absolutely a sports fan. I regularly attended University of Michigan football games while I was in Ann Arbor for undergrad and medical school, including the famous upset of Ohio State in 1969 described earlier. Crisp autumn Saturday afternoons in the 'Big House' with over 100,000 of my 'closest friends' was a ritual I fondly remember. I watched many of the other sports events on TV. I was a big college and pro football fan and enjoyed the World Series.

I was less of a fan of golf, boxing and soccer. However, the Olympics were 'must-see' television for me.

Sports were an important part of American culture during The Magical Decade. While some critics derided sports as 'bread and circuses' for the masses, sports teams and athletes inspired their fans. Sports teams unified countries, cities and states in support of their local teams. In the best circumstances, athletes served as exceptional role models for young people.

Sports teams also played a positive role in race relations, setting examples for integration and minority advancement. Some of the greatest athletes of The Magical Decade were African-Americans, including Hank Aaron, Muhammad Ali and Wilt Chamberlain. Among the championship Latino athletes of The Magical Decade were Roberto Clemente in baseball and Tom Flores in football.

The advent of the Super Bowl – the national American football championship game – in 1967 added an unofficial sports holiday to the US calendar, with Super Bowl Sunday rituals becoming an integral part of American society. In January 1986, my wife Claudia and I attended in person Super Bowl XX in New Orleans, the only Super Bowl victory attained by our local team, the Chicago Bears. Ever since then, I have regularly watched the Super Bowl on television every January (changed to February in 2022) – a tradition in my house.

CHAPTER 17

1965-1975: Pop culture - television

Popular culture played an important role in the daily lives of Americans, myself included, during The Magical Decade. Television, movies, plays, books and other performing arts added entertainment, education and occasionally enlightenment, through both traditional and new forms of artistic expression.

Watching television became part of the daily routine of many Baby Boomers. The quest for ratings motivated the three major networks; the higher the viewership, the more they could charge for 30- or 60-second advertisements. In 1965, there was only a limited number of stations in each market (for example, in Chicago, I could just watch ABC, CBS, NBC and the independent channel WGN). The Corporation for Public Broadcasting was founded in 1967 to produce noncommercial television such as *Sesame Street*.

All in the Family was my favourite television show during The Magical Decade. The situation comedy produced by Norman Lear and Bud Yorkin broke new ground as it featured controversial contemporary subjects including class, race, religion, women's liberation and the Vietnam War. Starring Carroll O'Connor as the bigoted Archie Bunker and Jean Stapleton as his long-suffering wife, Edith, the show premiered on 12 January 1971. Their daughter Gloria (Sally Struthers) and her husband Michael ('Meathead'), played by Rob Reiner, were the other main characters. The show became a hit during its second season and was 'appointment television' for me on Sunday nights. I liked it because it was innovative and funny, featured excellent acting, and covered otherwise taboo topics for situation comedies. *All in the Family* became the number-one show on television for five years (1971–1976).

It's unusual in the television industry to do a retrospective about a show still popular and on the air. I clearly remember, however, a one-hour television special hosted by actor Henry Fonda on 21 December 1974, at the end of The Magical Decade. The special marked the 100th episode of the show (there was another one after the 200th episode, which I did not see). Fonda narrated highlight excerpts from the previous five seasons, and there were brief appearances by the stars out of character. I laughed out loud during the highlight segments as Archie Bunker made outrageous comments about Blacks, women, Jews, gay people, war protesters and other groups. These had previously been forbidden topics in television situation comedies, but Lear and Yorkin skillfully made fun of prejudice and hatred through Archie Bunker's exaggerated, bigoted expressions and comments.

I enjoyed watching *All in the Family* weekly until it ended in 1979, but its legacy lived on in spin-off shows including *Maude, Good Times, The Jeffersons, Checking In, Archie Bunker's Place, Gloria* and *704 Hauser.* The original show had broken new ground for television with its biting social commentary about controversial subjects in the news at the time. The strong characters and sharp dialogue set a new standard for television situation comedies.

Star Trek, and its television and movie derivatives, was another television series from The Magical Decade that has had a long-lasting and continuing impact on society. Created by Gene Roddenberry, the first episode of the original series debuted in September 1966. The show was basically a television science fiction space opera. It told the story of the Starship Enterprise with its multiracial and multiethnic crew going on voyages of discovery in space. The theme of the show reflected the civil rights movement in 1966 by presenting a unique vision of an integrated crew exploring space together. *Star Trek* resonated with me because of both its space and civil rights themes.

"Space: the final frontier. These are the voyages of the Starship Enterprise. Its five-year mission: to explore strange new worlds, to seek out new life and new civilizations, to boldly go where no man has gone before" was the introduction to each episode.[78]

Lead actors included William Shatner as Captain Kirk, Leonard Nimoy as Science Officer Spock, James Doohan as Chief Engineer Montgomery 'Scotty' Scott, DeForest Kelley as Dr 'Bones' McCoy, George Takei as Helmsman Mr Sulu, Walter Koenig as Navigator Pavel Chekov, and Nichelle Nichols as Communications Officer Uhura.

Nichols was one of the first Black actors to appear as a major character on a television series. Dr Martin Luther King, Jr. and his family were fans of the show and he urged Nichols to stay on the cast when she considered leaving.[79] Nichols later served as a consultant to NASA in the mid-1970s as the space agency tried to recruit qualified African-Americans and other minorities to apply to the Astronaut Corps. Three African-Americans were among the 35 new space shuttle astronauts named in 1978.

George Takei was a pathfinder for Asian-Americans as a regular character on a US television series. Takei later came out as gay, but that was years later. Russian characters were also unusual on American TV at the time. American-born Walter Koenig was chosen to make the cast more international by playing the Russian navigator Chekhov. Nimoy's iconic role as an unemotional alien from the fictional planet Vulcan and his interactions with the very human William Shatner were emblematic of interspecies dilemmas addressed by Star Trek.

The TV ratings were relatively low for the original series, with 79 episodes produced spanning three seasons, from September 1966 to June 1969. However, the Star Trek universe developed a cult-like following in subsequent years.

Star Trek fans, known as 'Trekkies,' were attracted to its optimistic vision of the future, with characters from different countries, races and even species working together to explore the unknown. The franchise continued with a series of 13 movies, the first few of which included the cast of the original TV program. There were also follow-on television shows, including Star Trek: The Next Generation; Star Trek: Enterprise;

and *Star Trek: Discovery* with different casts than the original TV series. Movie sequels set in the *Star Trek* universe have continued to this day.

On a lighter note, Earth-bound television soap operas were a popular form of day-time escapism during The Magical Decade. Appealing to housewives, these daily dramas developed large, mainly female, fan bases that were extraordinarily loyal over the years. The oldest soap opera, *Days of Our Lives*, premiered on NBC on 8 November 1965 and is still on the air after over 14,000 episodes, although it moved to Peacock in August 2022. The drama is set in the fictional town of Salem and features the escapades of five families, including their love lives, traumas and adventures. My wife, Claudia, was an enthusiastic fan of this program, as well as another soap opera, *All My Children*.

While television as a form of entertainment gained momentum during The Magical Decade, so did the role of television as an important influence in American society. The 1950s had been known as the 'Golden Age of Television.' Shows such as *I Love Lucy, The Honeymooners, The Jackie Gleason Show* and *Leave It to Beaver* garnered huge audiences. The viewing market was dominated by the three major networks (ABC, CBS and NBC). By 1965, at the beginning of The Magical Decade, television had matured into a powerful force in the American economy, promoting goods and services, as well as attitudes and beliefs.

For example, television was a potent sales tool for the music industry. *American Bandstand*, produced and hosted by Dick Clark from 1956 to 1989, promoted the music and dancing of the latest pop musical hits.

Each program featured an in-person visit by a musical group. An appearance on *American Bandstand* could make or break a song or an artist. The Jackson 5, Prince, Aerosmith, and Sonny and Cher were among the many performers who made their national television debuts on the show.

I remember watching the show regularly to copy the latest dance moves and keep track of the newest Top 40 hits. The young people shown dancing on *American Bandstand* were usually clean-cut and predominately white, although the show did integrate in 1964 when it moved to Los Angeles. Some stations in the South protested, but Dick Clark was adamant about including some Black dancers.

Another example was the *Ed Sullivan* variety show, on air from 1948–1971. The show was appointment television for me and many others on Sunday nights. The program featured The Beatles in their first live American television show performances in 1964. While The Beatles already had several number-one-selling record albums by then, their three Sullivan show appearances in 1964 solidified their place as the world's leading pop music group and the start of the British Invasion (see Chapter 1).

During The Magical Decade, The Beatles appeared live on the Sullivan show for the final time on 14 August 1965. The taped show was actually broadcast 12 September 1965, and earned Sullivan a huge 60% share of the nighttime television audience, including me. This time The Beatles followed three other acts before coming out to perform "1 Feel Fine," "I'm Down," and "Act Naturally." Later they closed the show with

"Ticket to Ride," "Yesterday," and "Help!" Although this was their last live appearance on the program, the group later provided film clips of new songs to air exclusively on Sullivan's show.

Second, television became the mainstay to advertise commercial products ranging from automobiles to food fads. The Ford Mustang became America's most popular car in 1965 at the beginning of The Magical Decade, having been unveiled the year before at the 1964 New York World's Fair. A series of television commercials promoted the 'muscle' image of the sedan and celebrated milestones such as the 100,000[th] vehicle sold.

I earned my Illinois driver's licence in 1966 after I turned 16, but a car seemed out of reach at that time. I had to settle for using my mom's car, a Buick, when it was available. My parents were not able to gift me a car, nor was I able to get a job at that time to earn money to buy one.

Besides automobiles, television also promoted the latest food fads during The Magical Decade. In 1965, Franco-American came up with an idea for improving the sales of canned pasta in tomato sauce. Instead of long strands of spaghetti, which were awkward to eat, the company innovated with small, round pasta pieces that could be eaten with a spoon. They called it 'Spaghettios' and aimed the product at the infant's and children's market. Their ad agency produced a catchy jingle, "Oh-oh Spaghettios," to promote it and the tune still plays in my head when I think about it. The product was extensively advertised on television commercials with the tagline "the neat round spaghetti you can eat with a spoon." It became a big success and is a 'comfort food' to this day, with sales soaring during the recent COVID-19 pandemic. Most Baby Boomers, including me, have a few cans in their cupboards for when they need a fast, hot, tasty meal.

About the same time, in 1966, Doritos, the first tortilla chips, were launched by Frito-Lay. The original flavour was 'Toasted Corn,' but many others followed. Personally, I never liked Doritos, but they became popular, fuelled by television advertising. Frito-Lay marketed their new product with Super Bowl television ads after the annual US football championship contest began in 1967.

That year, 1967, was also when the National Football League adopted Gatorade as its official drink. The athletic drink had been developed in 1965 by scientists at the University of Florida School of Medicine at the request of the Gators' football coach. It was produced and marketed under the name Gatorade by Stokely-Van Camp to provide electrolytes, sugar and fluids to dehydrated athletes. Gatorade became the market leader for sports drinks by taking advantage of television ads, team sponsorships and celebrity endorsements.

Besides promoting music, automobiles and food fads, television during The Magical Decade was also increasingly sophisticated in influencing the marketplace of ideas. Importantly, political advertising on television developed during that time.

The November 1964 presidential race between President Lyndon B. Johnson and Senator Barry M. Goldwater produced some memorable television ads. Perhaps the most iconic was the 'Daisy Girl' ad. It pictured a young girl plucking flower petals with a countdown soundtrack in the background followed by an atomic mushroom cloud.[80] The ad was clearly recognized as an attack on Goldwater, whom the Democrats accused of being reckless about the risks of nuclear war. Produced by advertising agency DDB, the 60-second television ad changed political advertising from dull 5- to 30-minute policy expositions to brief, emotionally powerful pitches of ideas.

Public service announcements (PSAs) on television during The Magical Decade also addressed important public policy issues at the time and attempted to sway public opinion. In 1971, the 'Crying Indian' commercial created by the Ad Council featured an American Indian with a tear flowing down his cheek as he watched polluted landscape scenes. A voiceover said: "People start pollution. People can stop it." It was one of the most successful ad campaigns of all time.

Another powerful television PSA promoted the importance of higher education for African-Americans. The ad featured the now-iconic tagline, "A mind is a terrible thing to waste." The campaign was launched in 1972 to encourage Americans to support the United Negro College Fund. The PSA helped raise more than $2.2 billion through the years and has assisted over 350,000 minority students to graduate from college or beyond.

A final example of television PSAs attempting to mould public opinion were the ads attacking tobacco smoking before pro-cigarette ads were taken off the air for health reasons in 1971. In 1967, the FCC had ordered broadcasters to air anti-smoking advertisements on a one-to-one ratio with cigarette ads under the 'fairness doctrine.' While compliance was spotty, some memorable television and print ads were produced.

A classic anti-smoking ad featured a wrinkled older woman puffing a cigarette with the tagline "Smoking is very glamorous." Another ad read "Smoking kills your taste for life" with a picture of a large smoking ashtray filled with cigarette butts.

Thus, television played an important role in the popular culture of The Magical Decade. Television influenced what music I, and other Baby Boomers, listened to, what foods I ate, what politicians I supported, and my attitudes about social issues. I remember with nostalgia seeing Archie and Edith Bunker on *All in the Family*, hearing The Beatles on *The Ed Sullivan Show*, expanding my horizons with *Star Trek*, and listening to new music on *American Bandstand*. For me, it was a great time for television, as TV reflected the momentous changes in society going on around me during The Magical Decade.

CHAPTER 18

1965-1975: Pop culture - movies

Movie entertainment has been an American tradition since the 'silent movies' of the 1920s. Watching movies in theatres, drive-ins and on television has been an integral part of popular culture for Baby Boomers.

In more recent years, streaming has changed the movie experience, but as a child, when I still lived on the South Side of Chicago, on Saturdays I would catch a bus with my brothers or friends to the Avalon Theater. Built in faux Moorish style, this movie theatre from the 1920s hearkened back to that early era. It featured air conditioning (not a given for that time), huge screens and many rows of plush velvet seats (the opposite of the mini-theatres of today). Movie tickets at the Avalon were $1 and popcorn a quarter.

My favourite movie at the start of The Magical Decade was *Doctor Zhivago* (1965). This towering romantic masterpiece was based on the 1957 novel by Russian writer Boris Pasternak. It starred Omar Sharif and Julie Christie as individuals married to others who become lovers. Director David Lean used sweeping winter vistas and elaborate art direction to bring this story, set during the Russian Revolution, to life. The movie itself was filmed during winter in Canada.

The themes in the novel of freedom and individual rights were considered subversive by Soviet authorities and the book had to be published abroad, with some editions sponsored or even printed by the US Central Intelligence Agency. Pasternak won the Nobel Prize for Literature in 1958, but the Russian Communist Party prevented him from accepting it in person. The movie was banned in the Soviet Union and was not openly seen there until 1994. Pasternak himself died from lung cancer in 1960 and did not live to see his masterpiece translated to the big screen.

Doctor Zhivago's promotion of individual freedoms resonated with world-wide audiences, who at the start of The Magical Decade were looking for liberation from old societal rules. The movie was released in the US in November 1965 to mixed reviews from critics but was popular at the box office. It won five Oscars at the 1966 Academy Awards. The movie was nominated for Best Picture and David Lean for Best Director but did not win these prestigious categories. Critics said the movie was too long at three hours 17 minutes and that it was not historically accurate.[81] However, *Doctor Zhivago* was a box office hit and was the highest-grossing movie of all time for a while.

In contrast to love and revolution in Russian cities and steppes, *Midnight Cowboy* was set in the underbelly of urban America. Released in May 1969, the film was a triumph for Dustin Hoffman as 'Ratso' Rizzo, an ailing con man, and Jon Voigt as a would-be male prostitute named Joe Buck. In the movie, the two hustlers become friends in New York City, where they have a series of misadventures with other Manhattan lowlifes. At the end, they head together on a bus ride from New York to Miami, where Ratso hopes to straighten out his life. The sickly Ratso dies on the bus along the way in a powerful ending.

Midnight Cowboy was a critical hit and won Academy Award Oscars in 1970 for Best Picture, Best Director and Best Adapted Screenplay. It was the only X-rated movie ever to win Best Picture (the rating was later changed to R). While Dustin Hoffman and Jon Voigt were both nominated for Best Actor, they did not win. However, their performances were highly praised, especially Hoffman's.[82]

One of the top movies of The Magical Decade, and a special favourite of mine, was *The Godfather*, released in March 1972. It was a crime film based on the 1969 novel of the same name by Mario Puzo about the Mafia. The movie, a great success both among critics and the public, set a new high standard for organized crime movies.

The film told the story between 1945 and 1955 of the fictional Corleone gangster family. The movie focused on the father, Vito (played by Marlon Brando), and his son Michael (featuring Al Pacino in his breakthrough role). The film develops the character of Michael from a well-meaning young man to a ruthless Mafia don.

The Godfather won three Academy Awards in 1973 for Best Picture, Best Actor (Marlon Brando) and Best Adapted Screenplay (Mario Puzo and Francis Ford Coppola). Coppola was also nominated for Best Director.

In addition, Pacino, James Caan and Robert Duvall were all nominated for Best Supporting Actor. The movie was a big success at the box office and grossed over $245 million ($1.79 billion in 2023 dollars). The movie's gross was a record for that time (its production budget was estimated at only $6 million).

The movie and its two sequels in 1974 and 1990 became iconic. They elevated Francis Ford Coppola to the highest ranks of American film directors. *The Godfather* rejuvenated the acting career of Marlon Brando, as well as promoting the careers of Pacino, Caan, Duvall, Diane Keaton and Talia Shire.

The Godfather led to an explosion of Mafia movies and television shows in succeeding years. They were controversial because of their depictions of Italian-Americans as gangsters. They also loosened movie standards restricting foul language and extreme violence. However, high ratings and box office receipts, loyal viewers and strong critical reviews preserved their place in American culture.

In fact, at the end of The Magical Decade in 1975, *The Godfather Part II* won the Best Picture Oscar and Francis Ford Coppola was named Best Director. Robert De Niro garnered the Best Supporting Actor award the same night. The movie is both a prequel and a sequel to the original *The Godfather*. It tells the story of Vito coming to the US from Sicily and establishing his gangster family. The plot then jumps years later to his son Michael ruthlessly protecting the family interests after an unsuccessful assassination attempt.

I remember watching *The Godfather* when it was released and being impressed with its realism, intensity and pathos. I enjoyed the on-point portrayal of a Mafia family in the *Godfather* movies. The character development of Michael Corleone was an engaging story, with exploration of the psychological and sociological aspects involved in becoming a Mafia don. The violence depicted in the films brought intensity to the series. I agree with the proposition that *The Godfather Part II* was the best of the trilogy.

The glorification of violence in the Godfather movies was a sharp contrast to the 'peace and love' themes of the 1960s. The on-screen violence appealed to a darker streak in our characters, as well as the imperative to protect our families at all costs. The series resonated with moviegoers, including me, during The Magical Decade.

The decade 1965–1975 was a good one for the motion picture industry, with blockbuster films such as the *Godfather* series, and high box office and concession sales from movie fans such as me. This was long before in-house movie audiences were diluted by recently released films appearing on television or 'streaming' on computers and mobile devices.

There was something special about going to an actual movie theatre, buying overpriced popcorn and snacks, and becoming physically part of an audience. The collective laughs, groans and applause experienced by watching with others brought a feeling of community not available away from the movie theatre. I missed this camaraderie during the COVID-19 pandemic, when theatres were deserted. This sense of nostalgia for the in-person movie experience during The Magical Decade will hopefully return as life gets back to normal.

CHAPTER 19

1965-1975: Pop culture - performing arts

I walked into Chicago's Orchestra Hall and admired the magnificent classical structure designed early in the 20th century by noted architect Daniel Burnham. Orchestra Hall first opened in 1904 to become the home of the Chicago Symphony Orchestra (CSO).

The famed musicians began to warm up as I entered the large auditorium. We awaited the entrance of conductor Sir Georg Solti. Born in Hungary but later a British subject, Solti had been named musical director and principal conductor of the CSO in 1969.

I attended a couple of Solti's early performances as he began a 22-year tenure with the CSO, which Solti developed into one of the top orchestras in the world. Sir Georg was regarded by many as the most respected conductor of his time.

That afternoon, there was loud applause from the audience as the maestro entered onto the stage and ascended to the podium for a matinee performance. Dressed impeccably in a topcoat with tails, the balding, grey-haired Solti looked and acted the epitome of a conductor. Solti and the CSO were a precisely tuned machine, the orchestra exactly translating his vision of the music into a rich sound. His conducting style was dynamic and almost acrobatic. I remember Sir Georg used large gestures to conduct, which at times were almost jerky. His direction was clear and direct.

Although Solti and the CSO extensively recorded, it was a special treat for me to hear them live at Orchestra Hall with its excellent acoustics. The experience of hearing them live was so much superior to the sounds from an imperfect recording.

The CSO became world famous during The Magical Decade as Solti led the CSO on a triumphant European tour in 1971. There, on its first foreign excursion, the CSO gained many accolades and enthusiastic reviews as it travelled to 11 countries. Besides the European tour, the CSO under Solti won 63 Grammy Awards for classical musical recordings.

The summer home of the CSO since 1936 has been the Ravinia Festival in Highland Park, Illinois, just a few miles from my house. The park-like setting features permanent seats in a pavilion but also adjacent lawn seating where patrons bring lawn chairs and picnic. The CSO summer season lasted six weeks, while there were other performances during the summer by popular artists such as Janis Joplin (1970) and Ella Fitzgerald (1973). Every summer I attended one or two CSO or pop performances there.

Besides Orchestra Hall in Chicago, there were other important venues for the arts in the US during The Magical Decade. One of the foremost was the new

John F. Kennedy Center for the Performing Arts in Washington, DC. The genesis for the Kennedy Center was a bipartisan plan for a national cultural center, signed into legislation by President Dwight D. Eisenhower in 1958. His successor, John F. Kennedy, was an ardent supporter of the project, helping to raise over $30 million for the Center, and putting his prestige and that of his wife, Jacqueline, behind the funding drive.

In 1961, President Kennedy named Roger Stevens chairman of the board, a position Stevens would hold for more than 27 years. After Kennedy's assassination in November 1963, the project metamorphosed into a memorial to the slain president. The new president, Lyndon B. Johnson, laid the cornerstone for the building in 1964, but the facility did not open until 1971.

The plan was to use the venue for plays, operas and musical performances. The Kennedy Center Honors did not start until 1977, just after the end of The Magical Decade. Noted artists were feted with a medal and a special performance of their works at an annual gala attended by the President and First Lady.

The Center's opening night in 1971 featured the world premiere of Leonard Bernstein's opera, *Mass*. Afterwards, the American Ballet Theater (ABT) performed there for seven weeks each year in the Center's Opera House. World-renowned ballet dancers such as Mikhail Baryshnikov, Rudolph Nureyev, Gelsey Kirkland and Margot Fonteyn appeared in premieres of ABT productions there. Other ballet troupes that frequented the Kennedy Center included the New York City Ballet, the Alvin Ailey American Dance Theater and the Paul Taylor Dance Company.

Besides ballet and opera, the Kennedy Center was also home to outstanding musical theatre productions in the 1970s and beyond. Performances included *West Side Story* and *Candide* by Leonard Bernstein; *Showboat* with Donald O'Connor; Sandy Duncan in *Peter Pan*; and *Fiddler on the Roof* with Theo Bikel and Zero Mostel.

The National Symphony Orchestra had been founded in Washington, DC in 1931. Originally based at Constitution Hall, the orchestra performed frequently at the Kennedy Center after the venue opened in 1971. It was not until 1986, however, that the National Symphony moved permanently to the Kennedy Center. Howard Mitchell was musical director from 1949–1969 and was succeeded by Antal Dorati from 1970–77. Dorati, a composer and conductor born in Hungary, raised the calibre and reputation of the orchestra.

The much older New York Philharmonic was founded in 1842. Carnegie Hall was its Manhattan headquarters in the early 20th Century until it moved in 1962 to the Lincoln Center for the Performing Arts. Leonard Bernstein became the musical director, a post he held from 1958–1969. Bernstein became internationally famous as a composer, conductor, pianist, author and music educator. He was perhaps best known as the composer of the popular musical *West Side Story*.

Bernstein was succeeded by Pierre Boulez, who led the New York Philharmonic from 1971–1977. Boulez's tenure in New York was controversial, as he tried to introduce hitherto unfamiliar music to difficult New York audiences.

Across the country, the San Francisco Symphony played its first concerts in 1911. Under the leadership of Arthur Hertz and then Pierre Monteux, the Symphony performed and made recordings and live radio broadcasts from San Francisco's Civic Auditorium and, outside in the summer, from Stern Grove. Conductor Arthur Fiedler also played a yearly series of 'pops' concerts every summer at Stern Grove from 1949 through The Magical Decade. I attended a concert conducted by Fiedler at leafy Stern Grove during my medical fellowship in San Francisco, but I do not remember the details.

From 1963–1970, Austrian-born Josef Krips served as musical director of the San Francisco Symphony. He insisted on the highest standard of musicianship and did not record with the orchestra because he did not consider them good enough.

Krips invited a young Seiji Ozawa as a guest conductor, and the 'enfant terrible' gained praise from concertgoers and critics alike. Ozawa was named musical director of the San Francisco Symphony in 1970 and remained in that position until 1977 when he left to lead the Boston Symphony Orchestra. Ozawa instituted changes including a chorus, dancers and operatic touches for some performances. The symphony returned to recording with a contract with the noted classical music label Deutsche Grammophon.

The final great American symphony orchestra during The Magical Decade was the Boston Symphony. Symphony Hall has been the home of the Boston orchestra since October 1900; the venue was the first building constructed in the US with acoustic principles in mind. The Boston Symphony's summer home since 1940 has been the Tanglewood Music Center in the Berkshire mountains. The Center was founded by Serge Koussevitzky to teach young musicians. One of the first students was Leonard Bernstein, while famed composer Aaron Copland was on the faculty. The musical directors of the Boston Symphony during the 1960s and 1970s included Erich Leinsdorf (1962–1969), William Steinberg (1969–1973) and Seiji Ozawa (1973–2002).

Arthur Fiedler was appointed to lead the Boston Pops Orchestra in 1930 and held that position until shortly before his death in 1979. He was best known for his 4 July 1976 bicentennial celebration concert on the Charles River featuring a performance of Tchaikovsky's *1812 Overture*.

I was present in Boston on 4 July in a subsequent year to hear from the banks of the Charles River this inspiring piece with accompanying cannons and fireworks. It was thrilling to hear the Boston Pops perform the iconic overture in an outside setting with the loud coordinated booms of cannons and explosions of fireworks.

Besides symphonic music, The Magical Decade, from 1965–1975, produced many great performances in theatre and dance. I will give a few examples of my personal favourites. In each case these performances explored new ground consistent with the great changes of The Magic Decade.

In theatre, *Fiddler on the Roof* and the *Odd Couple* had the most wins in the 1965 Tony Awards for best plays. *Fiddler on the Roof* was a unique musical that explored how modern changes affected old Jewish traditions in a family in pre-revolutionary Russia. It won a total of nine Tony Awards – Best Musical, Best Musical Producer (Harold Prince), Best Musical Director (James Robbins), Best Musical Score (Sheldon Harnick and Jerry Bock), Best Musical Author (Joseph Stein), Best Choreography (Jerome Robbins), Best Musical Actor (Zero Mostel),

Best Musical Featured Actress (Maria Karnilova) and Best Costume Design (Patricia Zipprodt). The play was adapted for a movie in 1971 starring Topol as Tevye and Molly Picon as Yente. The movie won three 1972 Academy Awards, including composer John Williams' first Oscar for Best Score.

Both the movie and the play were especially meaningful to me because my father's ancestors came from a small village in Russia in an area variously controlled by Russia and Ukraine. I could imagine them going through the same dilemmas faced by families in the 1800s as old traditions came into question due to modernization.

On the other hand, *The Odd Couple* was a delightful comedy that explored the relationship between two old, cranky, divorced men. The play garnered Tony awards for Best Director (Mike Nichols), Best Dramatic Author (Neil Simon), Best Performance in a Play (Walter Matthau) and Best Scenic Design (Oliver Smith). *The Odd Couple* was made into a popular 1968 movie starring Jack Lemmon and Walter Matthau. It was later adapted into a TV sitcom starring Tony Randall and Jack Klugman that was broadcast from 1970–1974.

Perhaps my favourite stage production of The Magical Decade was the revolutionary play *Hair: The American Tribal Love-Rock Musical*.[83] This ode to the hippie counterculture, first produced in October 1967, was written by Gerome Ragni and James Rado, with music by Galt MacDermot. The play was anti-establishment, celebrating the long hair favoured by protesters against the Vietnam War. *Hair* broke new ground for American plays. The production featured full frontal nudity (not usually seen in plays of that era), profanity, references to use of illegal drugs, sexual scenes, anti-draft sentiments and a multiracial cast. A movie adaptation directed by Milos Forman was released in 1979.

I saw the play at the Schubert Theater in Chicago in December 1969 (FIG 19-1), and later the movie version (1979) and was moved by both. More than any other play during The Magical Decade, *Hair* epitomized the zeitgeist of the time for me. The music, lyrics and story were uplifting and high energy. The anti-war, peace and love themes were topical. The costumes and staging were direct from the hippie era. *Hair* embodied the counterculture of the 1960s.

FIG 19-1: Playbill from the musical *Hair* playing December 1969 at the Schubert Theater in Chicago from the collection of David Chudwin. (Photo credit - David Chudwin)

A half century later, I still enjoy listening to the soundtrack with songs such as "Hair," "Easy to be Hard," "Walking in Space," "Three Five Zero Zero," "Age of Aquarius," "Good Morning Starshine," and "Let the Sunshine In." There were major Broadway revivals of the production in 1977 and 2009.

Meanwhile, in August 1971, I was doing a summer journalism internship on the copy desk at the now-defunct *Cleveland Press* newspaper. I edited stories and wrote headlines under the watchful eyes of some veteran copy editors. One of the events I attended in person in Cleveland was the off-Broadway premiere of a new play titled *Godspell*. The musical told the parables of Jesus through the eyes of seven nonbiblical characters. The play was written by John-Michael Tebelak and the score composed by Stephen Schwartz. It began as a musical workshop at Carnegie-Mellon University but then evolved to off-Broadway (including Cleveland), New York and London productions. The song "Day by Day" reached number 13 in the charts in 1971. I found the play, and especially its music, uplifting. I wrote the headline for the *Cleveland Press'* review the next day. The theatre blew up the positive review into a sign, so my headline was visible from blocks away.

The Rocky Horror Show, one of the longest-running theatrical performances of the 1970s, premiered as a musical play in London in June 1973.[84] Written and scored by Richard O'Brien, the play has been a cult favourite for a half century. It pioneered on stage issues of sexual identity, with Dr Frank-N-Furter, a mad transvestite scientist, as one of the lead characters (acted by Tim Curry). The play was a take-off on B science fiction and horror movies from earlier years. After a short time, there was frequent audience participation during performances, including throwing rice at Brad and Janet, and dancing in their seats to the tune "Time Warp."

The play was adapted in 1975 to the classic movie *The Rocky Horror Picture Show*, which featured Tim Curry as Dr Frank-n-Furter, Richard O'Brien as Riff Raff, Barry Bostick as Brad, Susan Sarandon as Janet, Patricia Quinn as Magenta, Nell Campbell as Columbia and Meatloaf as Eddie.

The final year, 1975, of The Magical Decade featured Tony awards for two stand-out productions – *The Wiz* as the Best Musical and *Equus* as the Best Play. *The Wiz* was a soft rock African-American version of L. Frank Baum's 1900 book, *The Wizard of Oz*. The play opened slowly in New York in January 1975 but gained momentum and played for over four years and 1672 performances. The play was produced by Ken Harper and featured music by Charlie Smalls and Luther Vandross, among others. The cast, which was entirely African-American, consisted of mainly unknown Black actors and actresses. *The Wiz* won seven Tony Awards in 1975: Best Musical, Best Original Musical Score (Charlie Smalls), Best Musical Director (Geoffrey Holder), Best Choreographer (Jeffrey Faison), Best Featured Role Actress (Dee Dee Bridgewater), Best Featured Role Actor (Ted Ross) and Best Costume Designer (Geoffrey Holder).

An adaptation for the movie released in 1975 showcased major talent, including Diana Ross as Dorothy, Michael Jackson as the Scarecrow, Nipsey Russell as the Tinman, Ted Ross as the Cowardly Lion, Lena Horne as Glynda and Richard Pryor as the Wizard of Oz.

Despite its star power, the movie version of *The Wiz* was a critical and commercial failure.

Another notable Broadway play of 1975, the serious drama *Equus*, won Tony Awards for Best Play and Best Director (John Dexter), as well as being nominated for three others. The play explored the interaction of a psychiatrist, Dr Martin Dysart, and a young patient, Paul Strang, who had a sexual obsession with horses. The play opened in London in July 1973, but the long-running Broadway production over time featured noted veteran actors (Anthony Hopkins, Richard Burton, Leonard Nimoy and Anthony Perkins, among others,) as Dr Dysart. Younger actors such as Peter Firth and Tom Hulce played Paul Strang on Broadway.

The Magical Decade featured ground-breaking performances on the stage, ranging from serious drama like *Equus* to musicals like *Fiddler on the Roof* to campy productions like *Hair* and *Rocky Horror Show*. Orchestras in Chicago, New York, San Francisco and Boston achieved new levels of excellence. I was able to attend concerts in person of the Chicago Symphony under Sir Georg Solti, and the Boston Pops with conductor Arthur Fiedler performing on 4 July. It was a good decade for the performing arts.

CHAPTER 20

1965-1975: Pop culture - literature

Even as a somewhat precocious eight-year-old boy, I was a science fiction fan. I would go to the local branch of the Chicago Public Library where the friendly librarian would recommend science fiction suitable for kids, so-called 'juvenile novels.'

My favourite author was Robert A. Heinlein (1907–1988). He wrote a series of juvenile science fiction books in the 1950s that were popular with impressionable youths such as me. They were part of Heinlein's 'Future History' series, which outlined a fictional speculative timeline of possible events over the next centuries. Some of the novels in the series were directed at an adult audience, while others were aimed at young people. Heinlein grounded his timeline in an extrapolation of the science of his time. He was known for 'hard science fiction' based on plausible science rather than just fantasy.

One of my favourite juvenile books by Heinlein was *Have Space Suit, Will Travel*. It tells the fictional story of a teenager, named Kip, who wins a space suit in a cereal box contest. Kip goes on to save humanity from evil aliens with the help of Pee Wee, an 11-year-old girl, and a good alien called the Mother Thing. The novel, published in 1958, takes place mainly on the Moon. As with his other works, Heinlein takes pains to be scientifically accurate and his speculations to be believable.

Stranger in a Strange Land, released in 1961 just before The Magical Decade, was perhaps Heinlein's masterpiece. It is a fictional tale of a Martian-raised young adult who comes to Earth and interacts with human culture. Sex, religion, politics and philosophy are all examined through the lens of a young man raised on another planet in a different culture. I read the book in 1962 when I was 12 but did not understand much of it.

I wrote Robert Heinlein a letter asking about *Stranger* and about his background. To my surprise, some weeks later I received a postcard back from him (FIG 20-1). He wisely recommended I put away *Stranger* for ten years until I was older, as it was never intended for young people. He also suggested a book by Sam Moskowitz that included biographies of science fiction writers including himself.

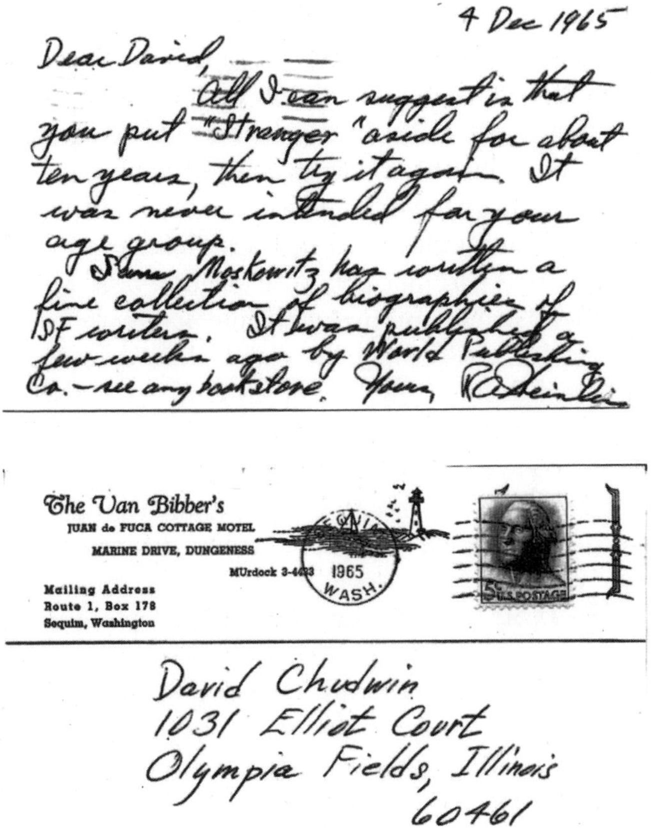

4 Dec 1965

Dear David,

All I can suggest is that you put "Stranger" aside for about ten years, then try it again. It was never intended for your age group.

Sam Moskowitz has written a fine collection of biographies of SF writers. It was published a few weeks ago by World Publishing Co.—see any bookstore. Yours, RAHeinlein

The Van Bibber's
JUAN de FUCA COTTAGE MOTEL
MARINE DRIVE, DUNGENESS
MUrdock 3-4[illegible]3

Mailing Address
Route 1, Box 178
Sequim, Washington

1965
WASH.

5¢ U.S. POSTAGE

David Chudwin
1031 Elliot Court
Olympia Fields, Illinois
60461

FIG 20-1: Handwritten 1965 postcard from science fiction author Robert A. Heinlein to the author in response to a letter asking him about his book *Stranger in a Strange Land* and his biography. (Photo credit - David Chudwin)

Besides Heinlein, my two other favourite science fiction writers during The Magical Decade were Isaac Asimov and Arthur C. Clarke. Isaac Asimov (1920–1992) was famed for his *Robot* novels and short stories, and his *Foundation* series. Asimov was a polymath who wrote or edited over 500 books. Considering that it took me four years to write and publish my first book, *I Was a Teenage Space Reporter*, I am in awe of his literary productivity. He is most famous for his Three Laws of Robotics, pertinent to today's debates over artificial intelligence:

> *"First Law*   *A robot may not injure a human being or, through inaction, allow a human being to come to harm.*
>
> *"Second Law*   *A robot must obey the orders given it by human beings except where such orders would conflict with the First Law.*
>
> *"Third Law*   *A robot must protect its own existence as long as such protection does not conflict with the First or Second Law."*[85]

His stories were scientifically sound, and his plots were logical deductions from basic scientific principles.

The third author was Arthur C. Clarke, a futurist who predicted communication satellites as early as 1947 as well as the author of award-winning science fiction novels and stories. He is best known for creating the story *2001: A Space Odyssey,* which was turned into a novel and the Oscar-winning, April 1968 movie of the same name in collaboration with director Stanley Kubrick.

I remember seeing the movie when it was released and was blown away by the plot and special effects.

I later wrote to Clarke, who was living in Colombo, Ceylon (now Sri Lanka). He autographed, at my request, a commemorative launch envelope for the first communications satellite placed in orbit by the space shuttle during the STS-5 mission (FIG 20-2). Many years later in 2009, the two actors who played astronauts in the movie – Keir Dullea and Gary Lockwood – attended Spacefest 2, where I met them.

FIG 20-2: Philatelic cover for the 1982 launch of the space shuttle STS-5 mission autographed by Arthur C. Clarke. The flight placed two communications satellites in orbit. Clarke in 1945 first suggested using satellites in geostationary orbits as telecommunication relays. From the collection of David Chudwin.
(Photo credit - David Chudwin)

There were many excellent science fiction novels and stories written during The Magical Decade. Each year the World Science Fiction Society gives the Hugo Award to outstanding works of science fiction in the previous year. The award is named after Hugo Gernsback, one of the originators of the genre. It is usually presented during the annual World Science Fiction Convention, also known as WorldCon. The first Hugo Awards were given in 1953.

The winners of the Best Novel category, during The Magical Decade and thereafter, were 'must reads' for me. A list of winners (published the previous year) included:

1966: *Dune* by Frank Herbert, tied with
This Immortal by Roger Zelazny
(both published in 1965)
1967: *The Moon is a Harsh Mistress*
by Robert Heinlein
1968: *Lord of Light* by Roger Zelazny
1969: *Stand on Zanzibar* by John Brunner
1970: *The Left Hand of Darkness*
by Ursula Le Guin
1971: *Ringworld* by Larry Niven
1972: *To Your Scattered Bodies Go*
by Phillip Jose Farmer
1973: *The Gods Themselves* by Isaac Asimov
1974: *Rendezvous with Rama* by Arthur C. Clarke
1975: *The Dispossessed* by Ursula Le Guin
1976: *The Forever War* by Joe Haldeman
(published in 1975)

With stiff competition every year, all these novels were worth reading, and I have read and enjoyed each one.

I also liked more traditional literature. My high school junior English class in 1966–1967 during The Magical Decade was an outstanding introduction to American literature. The instructor was Mr J.C. Dredla. He was a beloved teacher, known for his wit, sense of humour, love of literature and his painstaking evaluations of our compositions. He had a ready smile and a twinkle in his eye. I am in his debt for the writing skills he taught me.

Some of the highlighted authors studied in the course were Nathaniel Hawthorne (1804–1864), Edgar Allan Poe (1809–1849), Henry David Thoreau (1817–1862), Herman Melville (1819–1891), F. Scott Fitzgerald (1896–1940) and Ernest Hemingway (1899–1961). Each of these authors made important contributions to American literature and impressions on me as I developed as a reader and writer. These classic American novels originated in the 19th and early 20th centuries, long before The Magical Decade. However, during 1965–1975, I also read popular works of literature published during the decade. Some of my favourites broke new ground.

One of the most controversial novels of that era was *Portnoy's Complaint* by Philip Roth, which was released in January 1969. The protagonist of the story is Alex Portnoy, a Jewish-American bachelor, and his battles with his rampant sexuality and familial expectations. It is presented as a ribald rant from Alex to his psychiatrist. There are frequent sexual references to masturbation, including an infamous scene with calves' liver. Alex deals with issues such as commitment in relationships, his fixation with his mother and his Jewishness. The satire is sharp and biting. The overt sexuality of the novel, considered scandalous at the time, led to *Portnoy's Complaint* being banned by some libraries and schools.

On a much lighter note, one of the most affecting, popular love stories of The Magical Decade was the novel, and later movie, *Love Story* by Erich Segal, published in 1970. It is a tear-jerker that depicts the romance between two college students and their sad fate when one becomes fatally ill. The saying "love means never having to say you're sorry" became a ubiquitous popular tagline, although it was attacked, as was the novel and movie, as being saccharine and inaccurate.

Another favourite book of mine from The Magical Decade was Hunter S. Thompson's 1971 *Fear and Loathing in Las Vegas*. A contributing editor to *Rolling Stone*, Thompson was one of the founders of 'gonzo journalism,' the New Journalism technique in which the writer becomes personally involved in the story. *Fear and Loathing* tells the saga of a drug- and alcohol-addled weekend Raoul Duke, Thompson's alter ego, spent in Las Vegas with his 300-pound Samoan attorney. There is a blurred line between truth and fiction; the story is surrealistic, comedic, outrageous and ultimately insightful about American culture.

A drunk and/or high Hunter S. Thompson appeared at Hill Auditorium in Ann Arbor in February 1974 as part of a lecture series I attended. He personally signed a copy of his book for me before his lecture. However, his presentation descended into chaos as he ranted with slurred speech and needed to be escorted from the stage.

In contrast, in a more serious discussion, Soviet culture was explored truthfully and powerfully in *The Gulag Archipelago* by the Soviet dissident Aleksandr Solzhenitsyn. It was published in English in 1974 and had an immediate impact. The lengthy book describes in detail the origins, history and culture of Soviet concentration camps installed mainly in Siberia after the Bolshevik Revolution. The living conditions of the inmates, who were capriciously sentenced to exile for minor offences, were cruel and dehumanizing. The book was a great success both abroad and, in later years, in Russia after the fall of Stalinism.

Another favourite of mine was E.L. Doctorow's novel *Ragtime*. The book was released in 1975 at the end of The Magical Decade. A work of historical fiction, it includes both fictional and real characters such as Harry Houdini and J.P Morgan during the years 1902–1912. The plot revolves around a well-to-do family in New York and what transpires when they take in an abandoned Black infant and later her mother, Sarah. The baby's father, Coalhouse Walker, is a key character who plays ragtime music (hence the title) but goes on a rampage after his Model T car is vandalized. Race, revenge and discrimination are explored in the story that was made into a hit movie in 1981 and a musical in 1998.

I began my appreciation of 'literature' as a young fan of science fiction. Classic science fiction authors such as Robert A. Heinlein, Isaac Asimov and Arthur C. Clarke, brought the future to life with thought-provoking plots, engaging characters and a 'sense of wonder' found in good science fiction.

My high school junior English class in 1966–1967 was a more formal introduction to American literature (senior English was largely Shakespeare). Among other American authors, Herman Melville, Nathaniel Hawthorne, Edgar Allen Poe, F. Scott Fitzgerald and especially Ernest Hemingway had their own styles of writing and powerful stories to tell. Under the tutelage of our teacher, Mr J.C. Dredla, I learned paragraph and essay construction and literary interpretation. In junior English I honed my writing skills that were so important for subsequent college courses, journalism on *The Michigan Daily* and eventually book writing.

The novels published during The Magical Decade were controversial as befitting the times – they presented themes such as drugs in *Fear and Loathing in Las Vegas*, sex in *Portnoy's Complaint*, and tyranny and individual liberty in *The Gulag Archipelago*. They reflected the turbulence of 1965–1975 in many aspects of life.

CHAPTER 21

1965-75:
Pop culture
- fashion and
home decorations

There are time cycles in men's and women's fashions, as well as in home decorating and furnishings. Over a period of years and decades, what goes around comes around again.

One example of this is the widths of men's ties. At the beginning of The Magical Decade in 1965, so-called 'skinny' ties were the rage. Usually with a width of only two inches, these thin ties often featured wide stripes, large dots and odd geometric shapes. Popular colours were aqua, pink, purple and yellow. I had a few skinny ties, although in high school I rarely wore ties.

In the early 1970s, the tie pendulum swung back to ultra-wide ties with widths as much as five inches, more than twice as wide as the decade before. The ties were made of textured cloth, as well as the more traditional silk and polyester materials. Bright colours and designs such as paisley, animal portraits and geometric prints were the fashion of the 1970s. I personally had examples of each type (FIG 21-1).

FIG 21-1: Men's ties from the 1970s from the author's closet.
Note the wide widths, stripes, paisleys and textured fabrics. (Photo credit - David Chudwin)

The so-called 'Kipper tie,' first imagined in 1966 by British designer Michael Fix, popularized this new wide look into the early 1970s. According to Debbie Sessions, a blogger and expert in vintage fashions, "The Kipper tie was huge and came in bold colours, small feminine prints, and psychedelic swirls. It was meant to stand out and give the wearer true personality. The Kipper tie was literally the biggest thing to happen to men's neckwear in decades."[86]

Otherwise in men's fashions, suits were commonly worn by men in the early 1960s and not only at work but also in restaurants, bars and on aeroplanes. The suits were characterized by thin lapels, high-cut trousers ending as far up as the ankle and were accompanied by cuff-link shirts and fedora hats.

London became the fashion capital of the world in the mid-1960s. Boutiques on Carnaby and Lord Streets for both men and women featured designers such as Mary Quant. The 'Mod look' for men was popularized world-wide by British music rockers, most prominently The Beatles. They wore tight-fitting jackets with narrow lapels and four buttons in the front. Their trousers were slim and tight-fitting.

Over The Magical Decade, hairstyles got longer for men; moustaches and beards became commonplace. As seen on my school ID cards, I had a short haircut and no facial hair in 1965–1968. In contrast, by 1975 I had long, bushy hair and a moustache (FIG 21-2).

FIG 21-2: Evolution of the author's appearance during The Magical Decade from a crew cut in 1965 to bushy hair and a moustache in 1975. (Photo credit - David Chudwin)

The 'hippie look' beginning in 1967 and extending into the 1970s was a reaction to the formal suits and ties of the 1950s and early 1960s. The hippie look was characterized by bright colours, psychedelic designs and tie-dyed fabrics. Clothing for men featured patches, fringes, blue denim work shirts without ties, bell-bottom pants (flaring out at the bottoms, often with stripes), and floppy soft hats. I must admit I wore striped bell-bottom pants at the time; looking at pictures of me from that era makes me cringe now. Beads, necklaces with the triangular peace symbol, scarves and headbands were the most common accessories for males. Except for formal occasions, ties were considered passé.

In women's fashions, the miniskirt was the hallmark of the 1960s 'Mod look' for women. The birthplace of the mini skirt was London, where designer Mary Quant and others produced shorter and shorter skirts in response to the requests of young women. Quant gave them the name 'miniskirts.' She is also said to be responsible for 'hot pants,' the extremely short shorts favoured by trendy women in the early 1970s.

According to the blog Vintage Dancer, "By 1973 dresses were looking more like '40s and '50s fashion with A-line or pleated skirts and button-down tops. Simple one-piece dresses with a belt, cap sleeves, and swingy skirt or the two-piece tunic blouse, skirt and tie belt made up most casual '70s dresses."[87]

A glamorous style, exemplified by former First Lady Jacqueline Kennedy, was the product of famed clothes designers such as Yves St. Laurent, Halston and Givenchy in the early 1960s before The Magic Decade. Pillbox hats were commonly used as an accessory.

Women's pants in the 1970s featured wide bell-bottoms. Denim was the favourite fabric, but a variety of other materials were used as well. This less-formal look reflected the entrance of more women into the workplace, where more practical clothes were advantageous. However, palazzo pants, which flared out from the waist, were popular for more dressy occasions.

Later there was a dress-down hippie look for women. Tie-dyed T-shirts were worn, sometimes without a bra, along with military fatigue jackets, and either bell-bottoms, frayed blue jeans or long skirts that were ankle length.

While 1970s fashions may be laughed at today (especially the stripes and wide bell-bottoms), those of us alive then thought we were being very fashionable.

Besides distinctive clothing fashions, there were also home decorating trends during The Magical Decade. Just as clothing trends recapitulate, so do home decorating styles. Indeed, there has been a recent revival of interest in 'mid-century modern' furniture and interior decorating.

'Mid-century modern' refers to a style of architecture, home design and furniture that was popular from 1945–1969. The suburban house outside of Chicago my family moved to in 1965 at the start of The Magical Decade epitomized this style. There was a high-beamed roof with sharp angles; the kitchen featured glass doors, which brought inside views of the outside backyard; stone was used for fireplaces; and there was a flowing floor plan. The house was a ranch design with just a single-story structure that straddled two lots. While many of Frank Lloyd Wright's houses were designed before this era, Wright and his disciples foreshadowed mid-century modern architecture with their Prairie-style homes.

Inside, 'mid-century modern' kitchens featured open floor plans, wood ceilings, breakfast nooks, slate or other stone flooring, laminate countertops (with Formica being popular), and flat-front cabinets made of either metal or laminate. Larger kitchens had islands (sometimes with stovetops), while galley kitchens were used when space was at a premium. The era was characterized by use of bright pastel colours in kitchens, including yellow, green and avocado. Our kitchen in Olympia Fields featured avocado cabinets.

'Mid-century modern' furniture was sleek, functional and eschewed ornamentation. The legs of furniture were sharply tapered (FIG 21-3). Curves and geometric shapes were other common design features. Popular colours for furniture and fabric included tangerine, blue grass, wasabi yellow and red. This retro look in furniture is still popular; reproductions of 1950s and 60s furniture have recently become available.

FIG 21-3: Mid-century modern furniture included tapered legs and curved backs.
From the collection of David Chudwin. (Photo credit – David Chudwin)

It is ironic that some of the architecture and design from The Magical Decade has returned and is considered stylish today. There are copies at reasonable prices, but original furniture pieces from The Magical Decade can bring high prices. However, many of the clothing fashions of the early 1970s thankfully have not returned. These fashions have been consigned to the dust heap of bad designs, as epitomized by the striped bell bottom trousers and five-inch-wide ties which I thought were so stylish at the time.

CHAPTER 22

1965-1975:
Popular culture
- fads

Fads are defined in the dictionary as "something that people are interested in for only a short period of time, SYNONYM craze."[88]

The Magical Decade had its share of fads and when we look back, it's difficult in retrospect to understand why some of these crazes were so popular among us Baby Boomers.

Among the most outrageous fads were dances briefly adopted during 1965–1975. I do not believe I engaged in any of these funny dance moves, especially the 'Funky Chicken.' "Do the Funky Chicken" was a song written and recorded by American singer and entertainer Rufus Thomas for Stax Records in 1969. It became one of his biggest hits, reaching number 5 on the R&B chart in early 1970. Reviewer Stewart Mason later described the "Funky Chicken" as "the single goofiest dance craze of the 1970s ... While Thomas clearly knows how silly the entire concept is – he starts the record off with his impersonation of a cackling hen – he doesn't let that stop him from getting behind those goofy lyrics and giving them everything he's got ..."[89]

However, the Funky Chicken was not the first fowl-themed dance. Earlier, in the 1950s, there was the 'Chicken,' a popular rhythm and blues dance during which the dancers flapped their arms and kicked back their feet in an imitation of a chicken.

'The Bump' was another popular dance craze introduced in the 1970s. Two partners, generally one male and one female, bumped their hips against each other to the beat of the song. Sometimes the dance was more suggestive, with the female dancer bumping her hip against the male dancer's crotch. For this reason, The Bump is considered by some to be the forerunner of erotic dance grinding. Prudes in the early 1970s criticized these erotic moves as being immoral. A *New York Times* article in October 1973 was headlined, "Newark Dances the Bump, a Blend of Old, New and, Some Say, Risque." The story goes on to state: "'I don't want my daughter Bumping with the boys around here,' said Mrs. Clara Williams recently ... 'Dancing is fine, but the bump is just too suggestive.'"[90]

Another dance craze was 'Time Warp' based on a song from *The Rocky Horror Show*, a popular but controversial 1973 London, England, play written by actor Richard O'Brien (see Chapters 18 and 19). Starring Tim Curry, the play was one of the first to openly address transvestitism. "Time Warp" was an up-tempo tune composed mainly of dance step instructions, with the refrain "Let's do the 'Time Warp' again!" Audience participation at the play included attendees performing the dance moves in their seats. The song was included in the 1975 film adaptation *The Rocky Horror Picture Show* and the dance remains popular today, played at parties and weddings.

There were also fads for certain slang words during The Magical Decade. Some slang words or phrases have remained part of the language, but others have become outdated and have fallen out of use. The word 'groovy' is an example of the latter. Originally derived from jazz, a groovy record was one that was playable and musical, according to the *urbandictionary.com*.[91] The meaning was more broadly generalized in the 1960s and 1970s as something great, amazing or beautiful. Simon and Garfunkel's "The 59th Street Bridge Song (Feelin' Groovy)" from 1966 is an example of that usage. In recent years, groovy is the opposite – uncool and emblematic of the 1960s.

Another common slang phrase from that era was, "Can you dig it?" The question was used to ask whether someone understood or agreed with you. The phrase was part of the lyrics of the 1969 popular song "Grazing in the Grass" by the group The Friends of Distinction.

'Bummer' was another common word used during The Magical Decade to denote misfortune or a bad occasion, according to slang.org.[92] It was an acknowledgment of an unfavourable outcome, such as a bad reaction to illegal drugs. The word derives from 'bum,' or someone who asks for free handouts of food, drink or drugs from others.

A final example of a 1960s and 70s phrase is "sock it to me." The phrase originated from softball, where a batter would tell a pitcher to deliver a hard pitch to his glove, making a snapping sound. The phrase later was expanded to asking for a hard hit or blow. According to *urbandictionary.com*, "Literally means 'give it to me,' but generally had an underlying sexual connotation. Could also mean just give me your best."[93] The phrase became popularized by English actress Judy Carne and American comedian Goldie Hawn on the *Rowan and Martin's Laugh-In* television show, which ran between 1968-1973. The show was based on a vaudeville and burlesque tradition with quick one-liners including "sock it to me."

While fashions from The Magical Decade are discussed in Chapter 21, there were also fashion accessory fads. Puka shell necklaces were first produced in the 1960s from the apex of small snail shells found on beaches in Hawaii. The word 'puka' means hole in Hawaiian. These naturally occurring holes in the shells yielded small shell beads that could easily be strung together. These strands were then used to create necklaces. As their popularity grew in the 1970s, other types of shells and even plastic replicas, were used for these necklaces. Genuine puka shell necklaces became collectibles.

Later, in 1975, advertising executive Gary Dahl and some friends came up with an idea that became the collectible fad of the decade – the 'Pet Rock.' These were small smooth stones from a Mexican beach, which were sold in boxes with straw bedding, breathing holes, accessories and assigned fictional personalities. Each rock came with an 'instruction manual.' They were the top gift craze of Christmas 1975, at the end of The Magical Decade. Over the next six months sales, dropped precipitously but not before over one million 'Pet Rocks' were sold at $4 each, making Dahl a millionaire. The 'Pet Rock' was an example of a toy going viral even before there was a functioning internet.

Another accessory fad toward the end of The Magical Decade was mood rings. The face of these rings either contained liquid crystals or were overlaid by a thin layer of these crystals. The crystals were sensitive to temperature changes and changed colours in response to these temperature variations.

According to *howstuffworks.com*, "The colors are listed according to the change in temperature they represent, with dark blue being the warmest and black the coolest:

- **Dark blue**: Happy, romantic or passionate
- **Blue**: Calm or relaxed
- **Blue-green**: Somewhat relaxed
- **Green**: Normal or average
- **Amber**: A little nervous or anxious
- **Grey**: Very nervous or anxious
- **Black**: Stressed, tense or feeling harried."[94]

Finally, there were toy fads, some of which persist to this day. Hot Wheels are miniature die-cast metal cars. These toys were introduced by Mattel to compete with earlier, British-manufactured Matchbox cars. While Matchbox cars depicted commonplace sedans and trucks, Hot Wheels were speedier when rolled down a toy track and had bright colours and advanced designs. Both Hot Wheels, dating from 1968 during The Magical Decade, and Matchbox cars, invented in 1952, have been popular collector's items.

A much larger toy, Big Wheels, is a full-sized plastic tricycle for children that is low to the ground and therefore stable and safe. Many young kids learned motor skills and how to ride a bike by mastering Big Wheels. Big

Wheels was released in February 1969 at the New York Toy Show and was especially popular in the 1970s.

Another popular toy from The Magical Decade was NERF balls – soft foam balls that can be used indoors without causing damage to people, pets or property. (NERF stands for nonexpanding recreational foam). The concept was introduced by Parker Bros. in 1970 and continues to be sold by Hasbro. NERF balls now come in a variety of formats, including basketballs, soccer balls, footballs and baseballs. In more recent times, NERF water blasters have become best-sellers.

Those of us Baby Boomers who lived through The Magical Decade look back with amusement at pictures of ourselves from that era. Men in those times had big, bushy hair; long, thick sideburns; and moustaches or beards (FIG 21-2). We wore bell-bottom pants, sometimes with stripes, or blue denim jeans. Necklaces with the peace symbol were common, as were headbands. Women started The Magical Decade with miniskirts but later wore long dresses down to the ankles. Bras became optional depending on the circumstances. The hippie style was prevalent, with tie-dyed blouses and bandanas in some circles.

Thus, the 1970s had a distinctive look, both in clothing, architecture and design. The Magical Decade was a period of transition from the relatively calm early 1960s to the tumult of the late 1960s and the early 1970s. The unprecedented social changes of that era were reflected in the culture of the time, with revolutionary changes in music, television, movies, clothing and toys, as well as fads of that period.

Epilogue

The years 1965–1975 were a time of vast social and cultural changes, perhaps more than any decade in US history. I was lucky enough to be born mid-century – in 1950 – to be able to experience these changes as a teenager and young adult. In 1965, as The Magical Decade began, I was a sophomore in high school and had just moved from Chicago to a new suburban, 'mid-century modern' house.

I graduated high school in 1968 and entered the University of Michigan in Ann Arbor as an undergrad. I joined *The Michigan Daily*, the independent student newspaper, eventually rising to managing editor in 1971–1972. This gave me an opportunity to observe many historic events of that time. I entered Medical School at the University in 1972 and, while that consumed most of my efforts, I was still able to attend events, mainly in Ann Arbor.

So much happened in so many fields during The Magical Decade, and I was fortunate to be a participant or an eyewitness to many of them.

The Vietnam War was the central trauma of the time. President Lyndon B. Johnson escalated the war in 1965–1966 with rising troop deployments and American casualties. Like so many my age, I opposed the war and felt betrayed by Johnson, who had run in 1964 as a peace candidate. The University of Michigan was a hotbed of opposition to the war; the first 'teach-in' against the war was held there in March 1965.[60] I reported in person the

March on Washington in 1969 for *The Daily* when I was tear gassed.[58] In 1971, I again covered anti-war events for May Day in Washington as a reporter for *The Daily* and was almost arrested, despite being a student journalist.[59] I 'escaped' by running into the Smithsonian Museum of Natural History and hanging out with a dinosaur skeleton (See Chapter 10).

With a high draft lottery number, I was spared the difficult choice of deciding whether to allow myself to be drafted into the US military and possibly be sent to Vietnam. Five decades later, I still maintain that the Vietnam War was a mistake, based on false premises and carried out under wrongful rules of engagement. The military draft was capricious until the draft lottery was instituted, and there were still inequities in deferments afterwards, with Donald Trump and his flat feet as a prime example.

The Vietnam War had a profound effect on the politics of The Magical Decade. Johnson had been elected as the peace candidate in a landslide over Senator Barry Goldwater in 1964. Even though I was not old enough to vote, I volunteered in my neighbourhood to help LBJ's campaign. Yet four years later, his popularity had plummeted due to the war, so much so that he decided not to run for another term in the 1968 presidential elections. I supported the quixotic campaign of anti-war Senator Eugene McCarthy by volunteering, canvassing for votes and holding a fundraiser at my house.

However, the establishment candidate, Vice President Hubert Humphrey, became the Democratic nominee in August 1968. Antipathy to the war was a major factor in his defeat by Richard M. Nixon. Nixon pursued a policy of 'Vietnamization,' but this strategy proved to be folly. I was appalled by the bombing of previously neutral Cambodia. Furthermore, the killing at Kent State University of four unarmed American students on 4 May 1970 by Ohio National Guardsmen deeply affected me – it could have been me. After Nixon was forced to resign due to the Watergate crisis, the US retreated from Vietnam in April 1975 under his successor Gerald R. Ford.

The wounds of the Vietnam War persisted long after the US evacuated Saigon. There had been a deep divide between young people of the era who largely opposed the war, and their elders, who often supported it, at least at first. There was also a gap between traditional and hippie cultures, which the war had spawned, epitomized by the long hair, beards and marijuana use by the anti-war protesters. Returning Vietnam War veterans, many of whom opposed the war, were treated shamefully at times on their arrival back in the US; they deserved better from their countrymen.

While the Vietnam War was raging abroad, the civil rights movement came to a head at home. 'Bloody Sunday' in Selma, Alabama, led to the Voting Rights Act of 1965, which allowed more African-Americans to vote freely. However, *de facto* segregation remained a persistent problem, especially in Northern cities like my hometown of Chicago. 'Black Power' became a rallying cry and minority students on campuses demanded a fair shake in admissions.

I covered the historic 1970 Black Action Movement strike at the University of Michigan.[10] Ten percent minority admissions was 'assured' by the university's Board of Regents but never came to pass for a variety of reasons, most notably later Supreme Court decisions striking down affirmative action. Over half a century later, discrimination against Black people in policing and sentencing again reared its head in the aftermath of the 2021 death of George Floyd and other African-Americans by police.

The music of The Magical Decade provided the soundtrack to our lives. The 1960s started with American folk music but segued into the British Invasion, which dominated the second half of the 60s. The Beatles concert I witnessed in Chicago in August 1965 was a highlight for me, as were the three Ann Arbor Jazz and Blue Festivals I attended. Hearing Bob Dylan and The Band was another memorable experience. I missed the Woodstock music festival in order to cover the Apollo 11 mission (see Chapter 9).

Technology made major advancements during The Magical Decade. The first home computers and electronic watches were introduced. The US Defense Department established a precursor to the internet, called ARPANET, to allow computers to communicate. For my own medical research, I used computer punch cards to enter data into mainframe computers that occupied an entire room.

Computer miniaturization was hastened by the Space Race between the US and the Russians. During The Magical Decade, the US caught up and surpassed the Soviet Union in space. I was an eyewitness to history as I covered Apollo 11, the first Moon landing, from Cape Canaveral for the College Press Service and *The Daily*.

The Magical Decade began with a booming economy and ended with the double curse of stagflation

– a stagnant economy at the same time as rampant inflation. As a forerunner, there was a mild, brief recession in 1969. This recession was attributed to increased government spending due to the Vietnam War and Great Society legislation, Federal Reserve policies, as well as large exchange deficits with foreign countries.

A more severe and prolonged recession in 1973–1975 was accelerated by the 1973 oil embargo by Arab members of OPEC in retaliation for US and Western support for Israel during the 1973 Yom Kippur War. I witnessed long lines at the gas pumps with short supplies and higher prices for gasoline and home heating oil. While the oil embargo was lifted in January 1974, the lingering economic damage from inflation persisted.

Interpersonal relations also changed during The Magical Decade. Encouraged by early feminists such as Betty Friedan and Gloria Steinem, women fundamentally changed their place in society. Many women wanted more than their traditional roles as wives, mothers and homemakers. More women joined the workforce, but not just as secretaries, teachers or nurses. Women, in gradually increasing numbers, entered law and medical schools, and women started to take their places in executive offices and boardrooms, breaking through the 'glass ceiling' that had previously prevented advancement.

While the Equal Rights Amendment was not ratified, states began on their own to outlaw sex discrimination. Having been raised in a traditional patriarchal family, it took time for me to adjust, aided by my experiences at *The Michigan Daily* where intelligent, strong women were the norm.

These revolutionary societal changes were mirrored in my favourite television, movies and plays of The Magical Decade. My best weekly television program was *All in the Family*. The situation comedy, and its many derivatives, opened new ground in television by delving into controversial issues such as racism and sexism. *Star Trek*, both in the original TV series and later *Star Trek* movies, presented a hopeful view of the future based on inclusion, international cooperation and exploration. Groundbreaking movies such as *The Godfather* and *Midnight Cowboy* portrayed the gritty underside of America. Plays of the era, including *Hair* and *The Rocky Horror Show*, explored the fringes of US society. Controversial novels such as *Portnoy's Complaint* and *Fear and Loathing in Las Vegas* delved into topics including sex and drug use, respectively.

Professional sports in 1965–1975 mirrored some of these societal changes, especially regarding race. Two of the most prominent sports stars of The Magical Decade were African-Americans. Muhammad Ali recaptured and defended his world boxing championship, while Hank Aaron set a new record for career home runs in baseball, surpassing Babe Ruth's long-standing tally. Sports opened opportunities for acceptance and financial success for Blacks, Hispanics and other minorities. Sports also served as a unifying force for cities or states that supported their local teams.

Unfortunately, sports also provided a venue for violent tragedy, such as the massacre of Israeli athletes at the Munich Olympics in September 1972. However, the Olympics also provided an opportunity for peaceful protest as when American athletes Tommie Smith and

John Carlos raised their fists in a controversial Black power salute during a medal ceremony in 1968.

Looking back at photographs of myself and my friends during The Magical Decade causes a chuckle. I had bushy long hair, a moustache, long thick sideburns, and thick, black eyeglass frames. When I wore ties (rarely), they were at least four inches wide with either stripes or paisley designs. Casual pants featured brightly coloured stripes (FIG E-1). My female friends wore either blue jeans or long hippie dresses but were not into miniskirts more predominant in the mid-60s.

FIG E-1: The author in striped bell bottom pants standing near the Huron River in Ann Arbor in about 1975. (Photo credit – David Chudwin)

The Magical Decade was a time of growth for me personally and professionally. Between 1965–1975, I went from being a somewhat naive sophomore in a new high school to being a slightly more worldly senior in medical school, close to being a physician. I remained a 'nerd' but had accumulated enough life experiences and travel to become a man.

My time at the University of Michigan in Ann Arbor as an undergraduate (1968–1972) and in medical school (1972–1976) provided an exciting and supportive environment in which to mature intellectually, politically and socially. *The Michigan Daily* provided an opportunity for me to be an eyewitness to many of the events of the time, including the anti-war movement, the start of environmental consciousness, the space program, the Black Power movement, and cultural changes in music, television, movies, literature and fashion.

What are some of the lessons I learned from The Magical Decade? The legacies of both Presidents Lyndon Johnson and Richard Nixon are **cynicism about politics**. Johnson ran as a peace candidate in 1964 yet, after he was elected, he sent over half a million US troops to Vietnam with disastrous consequences. Nixon promised an honourable exit from Vietnam, yet he expanded the war to Cambodia and Laos and intensified the bombing in Southeast Asia, causing thousands of civilian casualties. Nixon's later cover-up of the Watergate burglary involved lies, misdirection and false denials.

This political cynicism is prevalent in today's headlines. The four years of Donald Trump's presidency were marked by a deep distrust of political and government institutions by his supporters. Their cry of 'drain the swamp' reflected a cynicism about Washington politics that has continued, especially after Trump incited protesters to march to the US Capitol in January 2021. The country was deeply split between supporters and opponents of Trump, with bitterness perhaps even greater than attitudes for and against Richard Nixon in the early 1970s.

Another lesson from The Magical Decade is an **aversion to foreign wars**. The Vietnam War started with less than a thousand US military trainers in 1960 and escalated to over half a million American troops in Vietnam by 1968. The US involvement in the Vietnam War was based on the false premise of monolithic communism as opposed to a local civil war between two Vietnamese factions. It was plagued by inaccurate intelligence, overly optimistic military assessments, and unclear rules of engagement. Before the draft lottery, American soldiers were drafted willy-nilly and sent to Vietnam, often against their will. The Americans there had to face a largely hostile Vietnamese populace, and a determined North Vietnamese enemy predominating against local military forces that lacked the will to fight. These factors all doomed the US effort.

While the situations are not identical, US involvement in Afghanistan, and especially Iraq, showed some similarities to the Vietnam War. The US invasion of Iraq in 2003 by President George W. Bush was based on the false premise that Saddam Hussein had weapons of mass destruction, and on a misunderstanding of the dynamics of tensions between Iraq's Sunni and Shia populations. Over 4,500 American troops died in Iraq before the bulk of US forces pulled out, leaving a weak central government and increased sectarian violence. The US draw-down to only 2,500 troops by 2021 created a regional power vacuum, with Iran gaining influence in Iraq via its Shia proxies.[95]

The situation in Afghanistan was even more complex. Afghan factions had been fighting each other for over a century before the 1979 Soviet invasion of Afghanistan, a neighbouring country. After the Soviets were defeated and forced to withdraw from Afghanistan, these groups again began to struggle, with the Muslim extremist Taliban party achieving supremacy.

After the 9/11 attacks on New York and the Pentagon, US troop strength in Afghanistan gradually increased to over 100,000 by 2011.[96] In that year, 9/11 plot leader Osama bin Laden was killed in nearby Pakistan by US special forces. The Taliban was initially defeated but then regrouped using guerilla war tactics.

The US realized that 'nation building' in Afghanistan was an unrealistic goal. Troop levels were reduced to 2,500 troops in early 2021 after a fragile and ineffective peace agreement between the Afghan government and Taliban was signed the year before. By the end of August 2021, US troops completely pulled out of Afghanistan and the Taliban rapidly took over the country. The Taliban were quick to establish Sharia law and discriminate against women.

Back at home, **expanding justice** during The Magical Decade strengthened US society. "Let us realize that the arc of the moral universe is long, but it bends toward justice," said Dr Martin Luther King, Jr. in a speech in August 1967.[97] One of the lessons of that era is that America's strength comes through diversity and inclusion.

The fundamental right of African-Americans to vote was won in the Civil War but lost during Reconstruction. Poll taxes, literacy tests, property requirements and sometimes violent intimidation prevented Black voters from having a say in Southern and border states. The focus on voting rights in the early 1960s was a recognition of the importance of concrete steps to permit African-Americans to freely exercise their right to vote. It took political pressure in the form of demonstrations and marches to force passage of the Voting Rights Act in August 1965 at the start of The Magical Decade.

Now, more than a half century later, attempts at voter suppression, mainly by some elements of the Republican party, are in the headlines again. Unfair redistricting, elimination or restriction of absentee ballots and early voting, and reduced numbers of polling stations in minority areas have been used to counter increased turnout by Black and other minority voters.

Demands for increased rights for women were also an important part of The Magical Decade. The passage of the Equal Rights Amendment in 1972 was a significant milestone. Even though it was not ratified in enough time to be added to the US Constitution, its approval by a majority of states led many states to establish their own anti-sex discrimination laws.

The 1950s paradigm of women as housewives and stay-at-home mothers was broadened in the 1960s as more women entered the workforce. Oral contraception gave women control over their own bodies, allowing them to choose when to get pregnant and the possibility of engaging in sex without fear of unwanted pregnancies.

Over the decades since then, more and more glass ceilings have been shattered as women have become astronauts, corporate executives, congresswomen and senators, and even the vice president of the US with the election of Kamala Harris in 2020.

Besides the fight to end discrimination against women during The Magical Decade, those years also marked a turning point for homosexual and bisexual Americans. The 'Stonewall Uprising' in 1969 was the start of the gay liberation movement, which sought an end to discrimination based on sexual orientation. This discrimination was later complicated by the acquired immunodeficiency syndrome (AIDS) epidemic. This retroviral infection at first primarily affected gay males beginning in 1981, just after The Magical Decade. I saw some of the first AIDS cases in San Francisco as an immunology fellow at the University of California San Francisco (UCSF). AIDS was called a 'gay plague' and was used as an excuse to discriminate against gay people in housing, employment, and access to public and private facilities. The development of highly active antiretroviral treatment in 1997, which made AIDS controllable with medications instead of a death sentence, was a game changer.

Gay rights is again in the news a half-century later with the Supreme Court having to weigh the competing issues of equal protection of gay Americans versus religious freedom as an allowance to discriminate. While many states have forbidden discrimination based on sexual orientation, and there have been US Supreme Court decisions affirming marriage equality, there is still no national protection for gay rights in important areas such as employment and housing.

Another area of recent controversy is tolerance for transgender persons. The Trump administration banned them from the military, a policy which was reversed by the incoming Biden administration in 2021. There have also been conflicting state laws and legal decisions about the rights of transgender people to use bathroom and gym facilities, and to participate in competitive sports.

Looking back to the 1700s, only white, Christian, land-owning males had full civil and voting rights. It is pertinent that the US Constitution itself specified that African-American slaves were only to be counted as three-fifths of a person in the US Census. Since then, rights have expanded as slavery was abolished with the Emancipation Proclamation in 1863; the 19th Amendment was ratified in 1920 providing for female suffrage; the Voting Rights Act of 1965 empowered Black Americans to vote; and the 2015 *Obergefell v. Hodges* Supreme Court ruling established marriage equality, allowing same-sex couples to marry. While the arc of justice has expanded, there is still a way to go.

Another important lesson of The Magical Decade is to **save for a rainy day**. The 1960s were a period of unprecedented prosperity in the US economy. The interval from February 1961 to December 1969 marked nonstop growth, fuelled by tax cuts and spending on the Vietnam War and Great Society. Baby Boomers who invested in the stock market then often became wealthy.

This era of good times with steady increases in the stock market came to an end in 1970. There was an abrupt downturn with the unexpected Arab oil embargo from October 1973 to March 1974. The stagflation that followed was a cancer on the US economy.

During 1961–1969, the stock market appeared to be unstoppable. Continuing new market highs led to a belief that no corrections would occur. Recent headlines promoted similar fallacies. Just as the stock market crash of 1973–1974 led to a drop of 45% of its value, some experts predict a similar crash is coming. In the meantime, it's recommended that investors diversify their assets and avoid overemphasis on growth stocks, despite their recent high yields. Commodities such as gold and silver, and their stocks, are hedges against expected inflation. Annuities provide a stable source of income, although their yields are lower and their expense fees are higher.

Most importantly, financial advisers recommend people have a reserve of available funds equal to four to six months of their income for emergencies. The COVID-19 pandemic of 2020 illustrated the importance of such an emergency fund, as millions lost their jobs and there were delays in providing federal and state assistance.

Still another lesson of The Magical Decade is to **be open to new technology**. At the beginning of the decade, as noted above, the only computers were large mainframe apparatuses that filled an entire room. Data was entered with punch cards and results were printed out on wide reams of paper. One of the first small computers with integrated circuits was the Apollo Guidance Computer, which first flew in space in 1966.[46] The computer's dimensions were only 24 × 12.5 × 6.5 inches. The computer had only a 16-bit word length and had random open memory of merely 36,864 words, less than the mobile phones or electronic watches of today. It was produced by the MIT Instrumentation Lab and was considered the height of 1960s technology.

Another advance in technology later during The Magical Decade was small Hewlett-Packard calculators. The HP-35, released in 1974, was the first shirt-pocket size scientific calculator.[47] The HP-35 was the first of a series of small, powerful HP calculators.

At the time, computers could not talk to each other. The approval in 1969 by the US Department of Defense of a computer network later known as ARPANET presaged the development of the internet.[45] It is hard to imagine now, but Baby Boomers like me had no personal computers, internet, social media or mobile phones during The Magical Decade, but the first steps in that direction occurred during those ten years.

There have been tremendous advancements in technology during the last 50 years, but one can expect even greater changes in the next half-century, so it behooves us to be open to these changes and embrace new technology.

A favourite subject of mine has been the evolution of space exploration during The Magical Decade. As explained in Chapter 9, up to 1965 the Soviet Union held all the firsts – first uncrewed satellite, first dog in space, first man in orbit, first woman in orbit, and first spacewalk, among many other records. The US began to catch up during Project Gemini with the first close rendezvous, the first docking, and the largest rockets in 1965-66. The Apollo program solidified the US lead against the Russians with Apollo 8's first orbit of the

Moon in December 1968, and Apollo 11's first landing in July 1969.

I witnessed history when I was present as Astronauts Armstrong, Collins and Aldrin walked out in their space suits early on 16 July 1969, and then I experienced, from only three miles away, their liftoff to the Moon aboard a mammoth Saturn V rocket later that morning.[49]

After years of competition, the US and the Soviets performed the first joint space mission in July 1975 with the Apollo-Soyuz Test Project. ASTP foreshadowed later international cooperation with both countries cooperating to continuously operate the International Space Station for the past 23 years. ISS cooperation has been a great success despite political conflicts at times during the two decades. However, the Russian invasion of Ukraine in February 2022 seriously frayed that relationship between Russia and the US.

In the future, new technology will dramatically change our lives. Artificial intelligence, gene editing, quantum computing, energy production from fusion reactors, nuclear rockets bringing the planets within closer reach, and nanotechnology are all possible, indeed probable, in the next 50 years. However, no one can predict the future and much of what has happened in the five decades since Apollo 11 was not anticipated at the time. Who would have thought after the last Apollo mission in 1972 that 50 years later there still would not have been a return to the Moon?

One needs to keep an open mind about future technology, be receptive to new technologies, and remain humble concerning our inability to predict the future. Change is inevitable and we should be prepared for it.

Another, less serious, lesson from The Magical Decade is to **keep the old clothes in your closet** because what goes around, comes around again. In men's fashions, the average width of ties changes like a pendulum. I have ties ranging from two inches wide up to five inches wide. The same is true of belt widths from one inch to three inches. Another example is the number of buttons on suits or sport jackets, ranging from a single button to five buttons. If you are a saver like me, keeping your old clothes long enough ensures you can always have something in style. There is perhaps a 20-year cycle in men's clothing.

There are similar cycles in women's fashions. During The Magical Decade, skirt lengths varied from the miniskirts of the mid-1960s to the ankle-length skirts of the 1970s. There are varying skirt lengths that have been described as follows.

- **Micro**: It is a skirt that has a thigh length.
- **Mini**: It is a skirt that is usually above the knee
- **Knee Length**: It is a skirt that is near the knee.
- **Below the knee**: It is a skirt that is just below the knee. While standing, the knees are not visible.
- **Midi**: It is a skirt that is calf length.
- **Maxi**: It is a skirt that is below the calf length.
- **Ankle Length**: It is a skirt whose hem is just above the shoes.
- **Floor Length**: It is a skirt that while wearing covers the shoes.[98]

Besides clothing, house and furniture, fashions have also recycled. As described in Chapter 21, 'mid-century modern' furniture and houses have come back in vogue.

Original furniture pieces from the 1950s and 1960s bring premium prices. Reproductions of period furniture with their highly tapered legs, among other typical features, have become popular. New sofas, bar furniture, coffee tables and chairs with that retro look are available.

Houses from the 1960s are in demand, especially those upgraded with newer appliances and new roofs. Ranch houses were common, and kitchens and living rooms featured open designs. Lot sizes were larger and there was an attempt to bring the outside in, with glass sliding doors and large scenic windows.

Another lesson from The Magical Decade is to **appreciate 'oldies.'** Music from The Magical Decade brings a sense of nostalgia to Baby Boomers (such as me) who grew up during that era. I participated in gym sock hops that featured music by The Beatles, The Rolling Stones, The Who, The Hollies, Petula Clark and many ·other English groups. Along with American rockers such as Elvis Presley and Bob Dylan, that was the soundtrack of our lives while I was in high school and college in the 1960s and 1970s.

There is also a continued appreciation for the television of that era. Popular TV shows such as *All in the Family, Star Trek, American Bandstand* and *The Ed Sullivan Show* live on in television reruns, and later in electronic media such as VCRs, DVDs and Blu-rays. Cable TV in the US has provided a variety of channels featuring classic television:

- ME **TV** (www.metvnetwork.com) The network, which is 24/7 nostalgia, currently has some 60 series on its schedule

- Antenna **TV** (www.antennatv.tv)
- INSP **TV** (www.insp.com)
- Cozi **TV** (www.cozitv.com)
- Nick at Nite (www.nickatnite.com)
- **TV** Land (tvland.com)

Besides channels with classic TV programs, there are other channels and streaming services with classic movies from The Magical Decade:

- Hulu
- Netflix
- Fandor
- Amazon Prime
- Classic Films
- FilmRise Classic
- Classic TV & Film
- Classic Film Festival
- Western TV & Movie Classics
- Classic Movie Vault

The literature, music, television shows, plays and movies of The Magical Decade have become part of the cultural heritage of humankind. Indeed, two gold records containing classic rock songs, including "Johnny B. Goode" by Chuck Berry, were attached to the two Voyager spacecraft that were launched in 1977. They visited the planets Jupiter, Saturn, Uranus and Neptune before leaving the solar system. Should some distant alien species ever retrieve the spacecraft, the records would help explain Earth, its history and its culture.

The years 1965–1975 marked great strides in my own life, including a high school diploma, an undergraduate degree from the University of Michigan, and my first three years as a medical student in Ann Arbor. I began my writing career as a reporter and editor for my high school newspaper *The Torch* and then *The Michigan Daily*, where I was managing editor from 1971–1972. I then developed an interest in medical research and patient care.

My appearance evolved from a high school student in a crew cut in 1965 to a medical student with long, bushy hair and a moustache a decade later in 1975. That year I was wearing striped bellbottom pants, which were considered stylish in 1975 but hideous now (FIG E-1).

During the same time, outside forces affected me and my fellow Baby Boomers. The Vietnam War, the civil rights movement, medical and computer advances, the Space Race, an oil embargo and recession, and cultural changes in music, television, the performing arts, literature and fashion directly influenced our daily lives.

I would argue that there were more changes in more areas during 1965–1975 than perhaps any other decade in American history. The Magical Decade was a remarkable time for me to come of age. Reviewing these events five decades later brings a sense of nostalgia, as well as pride. We Baby Boomers have been criticized by subsequent generations, especially by Millennials (born 1981–1996), but I contend we handled the challenges of The Magical Decade as well as we could.[99, 100, 101]

The term 'Baby Boomer' now almost has a pejorative tone to some in succeeding generations,[99, 100, 101] as if we claim to be the only generation to face challenges. Certainly, our parents and grandparents who grew up during World War II and the Great Depression, respectively, faced great challenges. However, I would argue that we Baby Boomers had to face revolutionary changes in virtually every political, cultural and social field, especially in 1965–1975. Mistakes were made, but overall we ended up with a more advanced, prosperous, peaceful, fairer and freer society than at the beginning of The Magical Decade.

I hope my fellow Baby Boomers have enjoyed this nostalgic trip back. I also hope younger generations who read this get an understanding of the events of the 1960s and 1970s from my first-hand historical perspective. I wrote this memoir in part for my own children and grandchildren to understand what I experienced in The Magical Decade during my formative years.

The more things change, the more they remain the same. Many of the political debates of 1960s such as voting rights, police brutality, abortion, affirmative action and sex discrimination have returned and are the subject of current headlines. So has the furniture, housing styles and oldies music of The Magical Decade. With advanced media technology, we can easily see reruns of movies, plays and television shows from that time.

It's been quite a ride, and I hope my own ride continues for some decades forward from The Magical Decade. It's been enjoyable writing this book to relive these events, which seem more like yesterday than half a century ago. I will let history decide whether me and my fellow Baby Boomers were successful or not during a period of unprecedented change in American history.

Timeline
1965-1975

(*Indicates the author personally
participated or witnessed)

1965

JANUARY
The first US football Super Bowl was
played as Green Bay defeated Kansas City

FEBRUARY
The military funded ARPANET to
allow computers to communicate
(internet forerunner)

JUNE
Israel conquered Jerusalem, the West
Bank and Sinai in the Six Day War

JUNE
The Supreme Court ruled in *Miranda* that
defendants had a right to an attorney and
to not incriminate themselves

JUNE
The 'Summer of Love' started in
San Francisco; the high point of the
Hippie movement

AUGUST
First space flight of the Apollo Guidance
Computer on an uncrewed Apollo spacecraft

OCTOBER
The revolutionary rock musical *Hair*
opened off-Broadway

SEPTEMBER
The television original series *Star Trek*
premiered, starting a cultural phenomenon

DECEMBER
First human heart transplant performed
by Dr Christiaan Barnard

1966

1967

JANUARY
Communist Viet Cong forces staged the Tet
Offensive in Vietnam

MARCH
President Johnson announced he would not
seek another term as US president

APRIL
Martin Luther King, Jr. assassinated, followed
by urban rioting*

APRIL
Stanley Kubrick's movie *2001: A Space
Odyssey* was released*

MAY
Author volunteered for the presidential
campaign of Sen. Eugene McCarthy*

JUNE
Robert F. Kennedy assassinated while running
for Democratic nomination

AUGUST
Author entered the University of Michigan,
Ann Arbor as a freshman*

AUGUST
Chicago police attacked protesters as the
Democrats nominated Hubert Humphrey

OCTOBER
Two African-American athletes gave the
Black power salute at the Olympics in Mexico

NOVEMBER
Richard Nixon defeated Hubert Humphrey in
the US presidential election

DECEMBER
Astronauts Borman, Lovell and Anders
became the first humans to orbit the Moon

JANUARY
Richard Nixon inaugurated as President

JANUARY
Philip Roth's controversial novel *Portnoy's
Complaint* was published

FEBRUARY
The Big Wheel tricycle toy was introduced
at the New York Toy Show

MAY
The movie *Midnight Cowboy* starring
Dustin Hoffman and Jon Voigt was released

JULY
The author covered the Apollo 11 Moon landing
mission with NASA press credentials*

AUGUST
The author attended the first Ann Arbor
Blues Festival*

NOVEMBER
The author was tear-gassed covering the
anti-war March on Washington*

NOVEMBER
The author attended the football game
when underdog Michigan defeated
Ohio State*

1968

1969

MARCH
The author covered the Black Action Movement strike at the University of Michigan*

MARCH
The ENACT environmental teach-in was held in Ann Arbor*

MAY
Four Kent State students were killed by Ohio National Guardsmen during protests

AUGUST
The author attended a papal audience with Paul VI and visited Jerusalem*

OCTOBER
The author wrote a four-part series on secret military research at the University of Michigan*

JANUARY
The television show *All in the Family*, featuring the bigoted Archie Bunker, premiered

FEBRUARY
The author appointed managing editor of *The Michigan Daily* for a one-year term*

MAY
The author escaped arrest during the May Day anti-war protests in Washington DC*

SEPTEMBER
John F. Kennedy Center for the Performing Arts opened in Washington DC

NOVEMBER
The movie *Fiddler on the Roof*, based on the 1964 play, was released*

1970

1971

MARCH
Congress passed the Equal Rights Amendment, but it was not ratified by enough states

MARCH
The Godfather was released, the first of a series of three acclaimed gangster movies*

APRIL
Jerry DeGrieck and Nancy Wechsler elected to the Ann Arbor City Council; they later came out as gay, among the first US elected public officials to do so

MAY
The author graduated from the University of Michigan with a BS degree in Zoology*

JUNE
Washington, DC police arrested five men for breaking into Democratic offices at the Watergate

JUNE
Hewlett-Packard developed the first shirt-pocket-sized electronic calculator, the HP-35.

AUGUST
The author entered the University of Michigan Medical School*

SEPTEMBER
Eleven Israeli athletes killed by Palestinian terrorists at the Munich Olympics

JANUARY
The stock market began to crash and the US entered an economic recession

MAY
The first of three crews was launched to the US Skylab space station in Earth orbit

JUNE
The Supreme Court in *Roe v. Wade* established a right to abortion (later reversed in 2022)

JUNE
The controversial play *The Rocky Horror Show* premiered in London, England

JULY
Peter Shaffer's play *Equus* opened in London with a later 1974 Broadway production

OCTOBER
Arab countries attacked Israel in the Yom Kippur War

OCTOBER
Arab oil producers embargoed oil exports to the US and other supporters of Israel

DECEMBER
Aleksandr Solzhenitsyn's *The Gulag Archipelago* was published in Russian in Paris

1972

1973

FEBRUARY
Bob Dylan and The Band played in
Ann Arbor*

FEBRUARY
Gonzo journalist Hunter S. Thompson
gave an aborted lecture in Ann Arbor*

APRIL
Baseball player Henry Aaron broke Babe
Ruth's career home run record of 714

AUGUST
President Nixon resigned before he could
be impeached for the Watergate cover-up

SEPTEMBER
President Gerald Ford pardoned Nixon
"for all offenses against the United States"

MARCH
The US economic recession ended but
unemployment remained stubbornly high

APRIL
US involvement in Vietnam ended
as Saigon was evacuated

JULY
Russian and US astronauts met in space
during the Apollo-Soyuz Test Project
(ASTP)

OCTOBER
Muhammad Ali defeated Joe Frazier in the
'Thrilla in Manila' boxing championship

1974

1975

Reference notes

1. Pollard, Kelvin and Paola Scommegna. "Just How Many Baby Boomers Are There?" Population Resource Bureau, published 16 April 2014.
    https://www.prb.org/resources/just-how-many-baby-boomers-are-there/

2. Paese, Meagan. "British Invasion," History of Rock and Roll, accessed 26 October 2023.
    https://thehistoryofrockandroll.net/british-invasion/

3. "Live: White Sox Park, Chicago," *The Beatles Bible*, published 20 August 1965.
    https://www.beatlesbible.com/1965/08/20/live-white-sox-park-chicago/

4. Gore-Langton, Robert, "The Original Bad Boys of Rock," *Express*, published 12 July 2012.
    https://www.express.co.uk/expressyourself/332351/
    The-original-bad-boys-of-rock

5. "*Billboard* Year-End Hot 100 Singles of 1975." *Wikipedia*, edited 30 August 2023.
    https://en.wikipedia.org/wiki/Billboard_Year-End_Hot_100_singles_of_1975

6. "March 7, 1965: Bloody Sunday," Zinn Education Project, accessed 26 October 2023.
    https://www.zinnedproject.org/news/tdih/bloody-sunday/

7. "Executive Order 9981: Desegregation of the Armed Forces (1948),"
    National Archives, accessed 26 October 2023.
    https://www.archives.gov/milestone-documents/executive-order-9981

8. "Brown v. Board of Education 347 U.S. 483," Case Text, accessed 26 October 2023.
    https://supreme.justia.com/cases/federal/us/347/483/

9. "Read Martin Luther King Jr.'s 'I Have a Dream' Speech in Its Entirety," WBEZ NPR, updated 16 January 2023.
    https://www.npr.org/2010/01/18/122701268/i-have-a-dream-speech-in-its-entirety

10. "Black Action Movement 1- 1970," Department of Afro-American and African Studies, University of Michigan, accessed 26 October 2023
    https://lsa.umich.edu/daas/engagement/gallerydaas/currentexhibition.html

11. Teicher, Jordan. "Why is Vatican II So Important?" WBEZ NPR, broadcast 10 October 2012.
    https://www.npr.org/2012/10/10/162573716/why-is-vatican-ii-so-important

12. "Archbishop Aymond offers '10 Ways Vatican II Shapes The Church Today,'" US Conference of Catholic Bishops, 1 October 2012.
https://www.usccb.org/news/2012/
archbishop-aymond-offers-10-ways-vatican-ii-shapes-church-today

13. "Nostra Aetate," Vatican Archive, 28 October 1965.
https://www.vatican.va/archive/hist_councils/ii_vatican_council/
documents/vat-ii_decl_19651028_nostra-aetate_en.html

14. "A Portrait of Jewish Americans," Pew Research Center, 1 October 2013.
https://www.pewresearch.org/religion/2013/10/01/
jewish-american-beliefs-attitudes-culture-survey/

15. "Christians," Pew Research Center, 18 December 2012.
https://www.pewresearch.org/religion/2012/12/18/
global-religious-landscape-exec/

16. "Religion," Gallup, accessed 26 October 2023.
https://news.gallup.com/poll/1690/religion.aspx

17. "What Is an Evangelical?" National Association of Evangelicals, accessed 26 October 2023.
https://www.nae.org/what-is-an-evangelical/

18. Olinger, Ted, "American History- The Autobiography of Malcolm X," *Key Peninsula News*, published 26 May 2021.
https://keypennews.org/stories/
american-history-the-autobiography-of-malcolm-x

19. "Scientology Controversies," *Wikipedia*, accessed 26 October 2023.
https://en.wikipedia.org/wiki/Scientology_controversies

20. Hayes, Lynne, "The Astrology of the Summer of Love," Astrodynamics! 10 July 2017.
https://www.lynnhayes.com/astrology-summer-of-love/

21. Kelly, Joseph, and Patrick Ryan, "History of Large Group Awareness Trainings," *Interventions 101*, 9 February 2020.
https://www.intervention101.com/2019/09/history-of-large-group-awareness.html

22. "Facts and Case Summary—Miranda v. Arizona," *United States Courts*, accessed 26 October 2023.
https://supreme.justia.com/cases/federal/us/384/436/

23. "Terry v. Ohio, 392 U.S. 1 (1968)," *Justia U.S. Supreme Court*, accessed 26 October 2023.
https://supreme.justia.com/cases/federal/us/392/1/

24. "Griswold v. Connecticut 381 U.S. 479 (1965)," *Justia U.S. Supreme Court*, accessed 26 October 2023.
https://supreme.justia.com/cases/federal/us/381/479/

25. "Roe v. Wade (1973)," National Constitution Center, accessed 26 October 2023.
https://supreme.justia.com/cases/federal/us/410/113/

26. "Dobbs v. Jackson Women's Health Organization (2022)," National Constitution Center, accessed 26 October 2023.
https://supreme.justia.com/cases/federal/us/597/19-1392/

27. "Roth v. United States, 354 U.S. 476 (1957)," *Justia U.S. Supreme Court*, accessed 26 October 2023.
https://supreme.justia.com/cases/federal/us/354/476/#annotation

28. "Miller v. California, 413 U.S. 15 (1973)," *Justia U.S. Supreme Court*, accessed 26 October 2023.
https://supreme.justia.com/cases/federal/us/413/15/

29. Nelson, Steven, "Drug Use Belied Beatles Squeaky Clean Image," *U.S. News Report*, 22 January 2014.
https://www.usnews.com/news/special-reports/articles/2014/01/22/drug-use-belied-beatles-squeaky-clean-image#:~:text=The%20Beatles%20never%20really%20were,boys-next-door%20image

30. Mansnerus, Laura, "Timothy Leary, Pied Piper of Psychedelic 60's, Dies at 75," *New York Times*, 1 June 1996.
https://www.nytimes.com/1996/06/01/us/timothy-leary-pied-piper-of-psychedelic-60-s-dies-at-75.html

31. "Book Review: The Teachings of Don Juan," *The Por Por Books Blog*, posted 31 August 2018.
http://theporporbooksblog.blogspot.com/2018/08/book-review-teachings-of-don-juan.html

32. Horne, Madison, "A Photographic Trip Through the Summer of Love, 50 Years Later," *History.com*, posted August 21, 2017.
https://www.history.com/photos-of-the-summer-of-love

33. "When You Come to a Fork in the Road, Take It," *quoteinvestigator.com*, posted July 25, 2013.
https://quoteinvestigator.com/2013/07/25/fork-road/

34. Schulz, Raymond, Jay Stein, and Norbert Pelc, "How CT Happened: The Early Development of Medical Computed Tomography," *J Med Imaging*, published online 29 October 2021.
https://www.ncbi.nlm.nih.gov/pmc/articles/PMC8555965/

35. "Half A Century in CT: How Computed Tomography Has Evolved,"
    ISCT.org, posted 7 October 2016.
    https://www.isct.org/computed-tomography-blog/2017/2/10/
    half-a-century-in-ct-how-computed-tomography-has-evolved

36. Qiu, Zhijuan, "Discovery of T Cell Memory," *Nature Portfolio*, posted
    6 December 2022.
    https://www.nature.com/articles/d42859-022-00036-3

37. Saxon, Wolfgang, "Robert A. Good, 81, Founder of Modern Immunology,
    Dies," *New York Times*, 18 June 2003.
    https://www.nytimes.com/2003/06/18/us/robert-a-good-81-founder-of-
    modern-immunology-dies.html

38. "Remembering Dr. Arthur Ammann," University of California,
    San Francisco, 17 August 2021.
    https://medschool.ucsf.edu/news/remembering-dr-arthur-ammann

39. Chudwin, Dave, "Wayne Morse: The 'ins' and 'outs' of Vietnam,"
    The Michigan Daily published 19 February 1969, page 4.
    https://digital.bentley.umich.edu/midaily/mdp.39015071754084/352

40. "Vietnam War U.S. Military Fatal Casualty Statistics," National Archives,
    January 2018.
    https://www.archives.gov/research/military/vietnam-war/casualty-statistics

41. "Report from Vietnam—February 27, 1968," *Voices and Visions, vandvreader.org*,
    accessed 27 October 2023.
    http://vandvreader.org/report-from-vietnam-february-27-1968/

42. Elving, Ron, "Remembering 1968: LBJ Surprises Nation With Announcement
    He Won't Seek Reelection " *National Public Radio*, broadcast 25 March 2018.
    https://www.npr.org/2018/03/25/596805375/president-johnson-made-a-
    bombshell-announcement- 50-years-ago

43. Nixon, Richard, "1962 Last Press Conference," Nixon Library, accessed
    27 October 2023.
    https://cdn.nixonlibrary.org/01/wp-content/
    uploads/2017/07/24093803/1962-Last-Press-Conference.pdf

44. Reeves, Richard, "President Nixon: Alone in the White House,"
    18 September 2001
    https://www.goodreads.com/book/show/19203567-president-nixon

45. "Paving the Way to the Modern Internet," Défense Advanced Research
    Projects Agency, accessed 27 October 2023.
    https://www.darpa.mil/about-us/timeline/modern-internet

46. Lomberg, Jason, "The Apollo Guidance Computer—History's Unsung Hero," *Power Systems Design*, 24 July 2019.
https://www.powersystemsdesign.com/articles/
the-apollo-guidance-computer-historys-unsung-hero/135/14863

47. "HP-35," The Museum of HP Calculators, accessed 28 October 2023.
https://www.hpmuseum.org/hp35.htm

48. "Altair 8800 Microcomputer," National Museum of American History, accessed 28 October 2023.
https://americanhistory.si.edu/collections/search/object/nmah_334396

49. Chudwin, David, *I Was a Teenage Space Reporter: From Apollo 11 to Our Future In Space*, (London, LID Publishing, 2019)
https://www.amazon.com/Was-Teenage-Space-Reporter-Apollo/
dp/0999187120

50. Wehrwein, Austin, "CREW OF GEMINI 4 HAILED IN CHICAGO; Rights Protest is Deferred in Honor of Astronauts," *The New York Times*, published 15 June 1965.
https://www.nytimes.com/1965/06/15/archives/crew-of-gemini-4-hailed-in-chicago-rights-protest-is-deferred-in.html

51. LePage, Andrew, "The Angry Alligator & the Snake: The Mission of Gemini 9," *drewexmachina.com*, posted 6 June 2016.
https://www.drewexmachina.com/2016/06/06/
the-angry-alligator-the-snake-the-mission-of-gemini-9/

52. "Parades for Astronauts," *Chicago Sun-Times*, published 27 June 1966.

53. Greenspan, Jesse, "Remembering the Apollo 8 Christmas Eve Broadcast," *History Channel*, revised 5 May 2023.
https://www.history.com/news/
remembering-the-apollo-8-christmas-eve-broadcast

54. Uri, Jon, "Dec. 27, 1968: Apollo 8 Returns from the Moon," *nasa.gov* posted 27 December 2018.
https://www.nasa.gov/history/dec-27-1968-apollo-8-returns-from-the-moon/

55. "Charles Duke Quotes," *AZ Quotes*, accessed 29 October 2023.
https://www.azquotes.com/author/37483-Charles_Duke

56. Roos, Dave, "Apollo 11 Moon Landing Timeline: From Liftoff to Splashdown," *History Channel*, revised 27 March 2023.
https://www.history.com/news/apollo-11-moon-landing-timeline

57. "A Look Back: Chicago Was Starstruck Over Apollo 11 Mission," *Chicago Tribune*, 25 August 2012.
https://www.chicagotribune.com/news/chi-110724-apollo-11-chicago-pictures-photogallery.html

58. "Washington in 1969 Hosted Largest Antiwar Protest in US History,"
    Stars & Stripes, published 15 August 2019.
    https://www.stripes.com/migration/
    washington-in-1969-hosted-largest-antiwar-protest-in-us-history-1.593314

59. Pearlstein, Paul, "Mayday 1971: A White House at War, a Revolt in the
    Streets and the Untold History of America's Biggest Mass Arrest,"
    Washington Independent Review of Books, published 13 August 2020.
    https://www.washingtonindependentreviewofbooks.com/index.php/
    bookreview/mayday-1971-a-white-house-at-war-a-revolt-in-the-streets-and-
    the-untold-history-of-americas-biggest-mass-arrest

60. Glenn, Alan, "Teach-in + 50," *Michigan Today*, posted 16 March 2015.
    https://michigantoday.umich.edu/2015/03/16/teach-in-50/

61. "National Mobilization Committee to End the War in Vietnam," *Wikipedia*,
    last edited 25 September 2023.
    https://en.wikipedia.org/wiki/
    National_Mobilization_Committee_to_End_the_War_in_Vietnam

62. Taylor, David, and Sam Morris, "The Whole World is Watching,"
    The Guardian, published 19 August 2018.
    https://www.theguardian.com/us-news/ng-interactive/2018/aug/19/
    the-whole-world-is-watching-chicago-police-riot-vietnam-war-regan

63. "Moratorium to End the War in Vietnam," *Wikipedia*, last edited
    27 September 2023.
    https://en.wikipedia.org/wiki/Moratorium_to_End_the_War_in_Vietnam

64. Zhang, Michael, "The Kent State Massacre Photo and the Case of the Missing
    Pole," *PetaPixel*, posted 29 August 2012.
    https://petapixel.com/2012/08/29/
    the-kent-state-massacre-photo-and-the-case-of-the-missing-pole/

65. "The Kent State Tragedy, by The President's Commission on Campus
    Unrest," Kent State University Libraries, published October 1970.
    https://omeka.library.kent.edu/special-collections/items/show/3419

66. Hutchinson, Lydia, "Neil Young's Ohio," *Performing Songwriter*, posted
    4 May 2017.
    https://performingsongwriter.com/neil-young-ohio/

67. Chudwin, Dave, "'U 'Research: Bringing the War Home," *The Michigan Daily*,
    published 27 October 1970.
    https://digital.bentley.umich.edu/midaily/mdp.39015071754423/477

68. Chudwin, Dave, "Electronic Battlefield: 'U' and the Indochina War,"
    The Michigan Daily, published 9 March 1971.
    https://digital.bentley.umich.edu/midaily/mdp.39015071754415/413

69. "Openness in Research Contracts, Grants, and Agreements," *U-M Standard Practice Guide*, issued 17 February 1993.
https://spg.umich.edu/policy/303.01

70. Chudwin, Dave, "50,000 Participate in 'U' Environmental Teach-in," *The Michigan Daily*, published 2 September 1970.
https://digital.bentley.umich.edu/midaily/mdp.39015071754423/16

71. Cohen, Alex and Wilfred Codrington III, "The Equal Rights Amendment Explained," Brennan Center for Justice, posted 23 January 2020.
https://www.brennancenter.org/our-work/research-reports/equal-rights-amendment-explained?ref=popsugar.com

72. "A Timeline of Contraception," American Experience, Public Broadcasting System, accessed 1 November 2023.
https://www.pbs.org/wgbh/americanexperience/features/pill-timeline/

73. "Lawrence v. Texas, 539 U.S. 558 (2003), *Justia U.S. Supreme Court*, 26 June 2003.
https://supreme.justia.com/cases/federal/us/539/558/

74. Smith, Laura, "When LBJ's Closest Aide Was Caught in a Gay Sex Sting, the President Caved—the First Lady Stood Up," *Timeline*, 28 September 2017.
https://timeline.com/walter-jenkins-gay-lbj-21d71a731021

75. Fredrickson, Caroline and Ilan Wurman, "Obergefell v. Hodges," Constitution Center, 2015.
https://supreme.justia.com/cases/federal/us/576/14-556/

76. Fost, Norman and David Chudwin and Daniel Wikler, "The Limited Moral Significance of 'Fetal Viability,'" *Hastings Center Report* 10 (6): 10-13 (1980).

77. "Planned Parenthood of Southeastern Pa. v. Casey, 505 U.S. 833 (1992)," *Justia U.S. Supreme Court*, 1992.
https://supreme.justia.com/cases/federal/us/505/833/

78. "Star Trek Opening," *Genius*, 8 September 1966.
https://genius.com/Star-trek-star-trek-opening-lyrics

79. Dagan, Carmel, "Nichelle Nichols, Uhura in 'Star Trek,' Dies at 89," *Variety*, posted 21 July 2022.
https://variety.com/2022/tv/news/nichelle-nichols-dead-star-trek-the-original-series-1235330159/

80. Mann, Robert, "How the "Daisy" Ad Changed Everything About Political Advertising," *Smithsonian Magazine*, 13 April 2016.
https://www.smithsonianmag.com/history/how-daisy-ad-changed-everything-about-political-advertising-180958741/

81. "Dr. Zhivago," *IMDb*, accessed 31 October 2023.
    https://www.imdb.com/title/tt0059113/

82. Ebert, Roger, "Midnight Cowboy" *RogerEbert.com*, posted 4 July 1994.
    https://www.rogerebert.com/reviews/midnight-cowboy-1969

83. Lee, Sarah, "Hair: The Musical that 'Changed Theatre Forever,'"
    BBC, broadcast 27 September 2018.
    https://www.bbc.com/news/uk-england-london-45625785

84. "The Rocky Horror Show," *Wikipedia*, accessed 31 October 2023.
    https://en.wikipedia.org/wiki/The_Rocky_Horror_Show

85. "What are Isaac Asimov's three laws of robotics?" Notes and Queries,
    The Guardian, accessed 31 October 2023.
    https://www.theguardian.com/notesandqueries/query/0,5753,-21259,00.html

86. Sessions, Debbie, "Vintage Men's Tie History 1920-1970," *Vintage Dancer*,
    posted 14 November 2012.
    https://vintagedancer.com/vintage/mens-tie-history-1920s-to-1970s/

87. Sessions, Debbie, "1970s Dress Styles – 70s Dress Fashion History,"
    Vintage Dancer, posted 10 October 2018.
    https://vintagedancer.com/1970s/1970s-dress-styles/

88. "Fad," *Oxford Learners Dictionaries*, accessed 1 November 2023.
    www.oxfordlearnersdictionaries.com/us/definition/english/fad

89. Mason, Stewart, "Do the Funky Chicken Review by Stewart Mason,"
    allmusic.com, accessed 1 November 2023.
    https://www.allmusic.com/song/do-the-funky-chicken-mt0010787968#review

90. Smith, Welton, "Newark Dances the Bump, a Blend Of Old, New and, Some
    Say, Risque," *New York Times*, published 7 October 1973.
    https://www.nytimes.com/1973/10/07/archives/newark-dances-the-bump-a-
    blend-of-old-new-and-some-say-risque.html

91. "Groovy," Urban Dictionary," accessed 1 November 2023.
    https://www.urbandictionary.com/define.php?term=groovy

92. "What Does Bummer Mean?" *slang.org*, accessed 2 November 2023.
    https://www.slang.org/bummer-meaning-definition/

93. ambrosia, "Sock it to me," *Urban Dictionary*, posted 30 June 2009.
    https://www.urbandictionary.com/define.php?term=Sock%20it%20to%20me

94. "What's the Science Behind Mood Rings?" *howstuffworks.com*, updated
    24 April 2023.
    https://people.howstuffworks.com/mood-rings.htm

95. Hamasaeed, Sarhang and Garrett, Nada, "Iraq Timeline: Since the 2003 War," United States Institute of Peace, posted 29 May 2020. https://www.usip.org/iraq-timeline-2003-war

96. "War in Afghanistan (2001-2021)" *Wikipedia*, last edited 20 October 2023. https://en.wikipedia.org/wiki/War_in_Afghanistan_(2001%E2%80%932021)

97. King, Martin Luther, "Quotations" Martin Luther King, Jr. Memorial website, accessed 25 November 2023. https://www.nps.gov/mlkm/learn/quotations.htm

98. "Hemline" *Wikipedia*, last edited 19 October 2023. https://en.wikipedia.org/wiki/Hemline

99. Fanlund, Paul, "Paul Fanlund Baby Boomers Are the Worst Generation Ever, or So We're Told," *The Cap Times*, published 16 April 2021. https://captimes.com/opinion/column/paul_fanlund/paul-fanlund-baby-boomers-are-the-worst-generation-ever-or-so-we-re-told/article_8b78d415-1ee4-5c5e-93e3-b60b231828e1.html

100. Getlen, Larry. "Why Millennials' Distaste for Baby Boomers is Justified," *New York Post,* published 11 August 2020. https://nypost.com/2020/08/08/why-millenials-distaste-for-baby-boomers-is-justified

101. Wallace-Wells, Benjamin, "The Conservative Case Against the Boomers," *The New Yorker,* published 28 January 2021. https://www.newyorker.com/news/our-columnists/the-conservative-case-against-the-boomers

Index

Acknowledgements

Writing is often a solitary effort, but input from family, friends and colleagues can prove invaluable. I am especially grateful to the following individuals for suggestions, corrections and advice about the manuscript for this book: (alphabetically) Gail Becker, John Bisney, Adam Chudwin, Francis French, Stacy Lamkin and Marvin Rubenstein.

I would also like to thank the following successful authors and journalists for reading the final manuscript and writing the Advance Praises that appear on the back and interior covers: John Bisney, Francis French, James R. Hansen, Peter King, Robert Kurson, Marvin Rubenstein and John Zarrella.

The team at LID Publishing has been very professional and helpful. I thank Publisher, Martin Liu, and Editorial Director, Clare Christian, for accepting my manuscript. Literary consultant and author, Susan Furber, structurally edited the manuscript for LID and did an outstanding job helping me focus the book. Caroline Li is responsible for the cover and interior design, including the visually striking Timeline. Thanks also to Shazia Fardous, who copyedited the manuscript, and Jody Amato for proofreading it.

This book is dedicated to my family for all their support and encouragement, especially to my son, Adam, my daughter, Stacy Lamkin, and to my sweet granddaughter, Callie. Although she did not live to see the final product, my late wife, Claudia, encouraged me to take on this memoir of an earlier era. I hope this book informs and educates them, giving them a look at the changes and challenges I and other Baby Boomers experienced during 1965–1975.